EAT THE APPLE

Matt Young

BLOOMSBURY
LONDON · OXFORD · NEW YORK · NEW DELHI · SYDNEY

Bloomsbury Publishing
An imprint of Bloomsbury Publishing Plc

50 Bedford Square
London
WC1B 3DP
UK

1385 Broadway
New York
NY 10018
USA

www.bloomsbury.com

BLOOMSBURY and the Diana logo are trademarks of Bloomsbury Publishing Plc

First published in Great Britain 2018
© Matt Young, 2018

British Library Cataloguing-in-Publication Data
A catalogue record for this book is available from the British Library.

ISBN: HB: 978-1-4088-8828-5
TPB: 978-1-4088-8829-2
ePub: 978-1-4088-8826-1

2 4 6 8 10 9 7 5 3 1

Typeset by Westchester Publishing Services
Printed and bound in Great Britain by CPI Group (UK) Ltd, Croydon CR0 4YY

To find out more about our authors and books visit www.bloomsbury.com. Here you will find extracts, author interviews, details of forthcoming events and the option to sign up for our newsletters.

For my grandfather

Eat the Apple. Fuck the Corps.

—Marine Corps Proverb

Choose Your Own Adventure

IN FEBRUARY 2005 AT AN armed forces recruitment center situated between a Pier 1 Imports and a Walmart, in the middle of a strip mall of miscellanea, a Marine Corps recruiter goes over your Armed Services Vocational Aptitude Battery and says you scored high and to take your pick of jobs.

To decide that maybe this was all a mistake, turn around, and walk out of the recruiter's office with no hard feelings, and instead continue your menial-labor job and join the union and marry the girl you're dating and have kids and buy a house in the Midwest and get divorced and hate your job and your ex-wife and never speak to your kids and develop a drinking problem no one wants to talk about because you insist you don't have a problem and burn bridges with anyone who insinuates said drinking problem exists and start voting against your best interests and think maybe it really is the immigrants' fault and the liberals' fault and buy a bumper sticker that reads AMERICA: LOVE IT OR LEAVE IT and believe it, stop reading and go about your day.

To join the United States Marine Corps infantry, proceed to the next page.

You've chosen the United States Marine Corps infantry based on one thing: You got drunk last night and crashed your car into a fire hydrant sometime in the early morning and think—because your idea of masculinity is severely twisted and damaged by the male figures in your life and the media with which you surround yourself—that the only way to change is the self-flagellation achieved by signing up for war.

You will ship out for recruit training to San Diego, California, in April 2005. Your family—broken and distant—will remain silent as to your decision. Only an ex-girlfriend, with whom you're still in contact, will beg you not to go with words of oil and death and futility. You'll wish you'd listened.

Your experience will not be what you think. You wear glasses. Heroes don't wear glasses. Clark Kent wears glasses—he's an alter ego, an alien's perception of the weakness, ineffectuality, and cowardice of the human race. All the men who wear glasses in movies are expendable: They don't get the girl; they don't redeem themselves. They are the loners or villains.

You will become the villain.

When a drill instructor steps on your glasses you will be able to do nothing except look through broken portholes for weeks. When the brainstrap holding the glasses to your face rubs the skin behind your ears raw, you will not be able to remove them—without them you would be blind. Because you didn't think about the need to wear glasses they will come to stand for everything you do not know, and for that you will hate them. You will replace them with contacts, hiding the problem, faking your way through it. No one will see them, but they will be there.

You will be exploded and shot at and made a fool of and hated and feared and loved and fellated and fucked and lonely and tired and suicidal.

Because you feel abandoned by your father you will look for a father figure in a sea of similarly uniformed men and you will find many. These men will berate you and beat you and break you, but they won't leave you. Years from meeting them you will not be able to sleep at night as you replay the ways in which you let them down, or might have let them down, in your head. You will lie in bed and your face will grow hot and your heart will thud in your chest and your skin will crawl and you will feel ashamed. Because you are a son to those men and shame is what sons feel in the presence of their fathers, and those fathers will be with you always. You will be a father to other men like you. They will suffer the same fate.

You will estrange yourself from your mother. You will blame her for your choices. Your knees will ache and nerves in your neck will misfire. You will break knuckles in drunken brawls and suffer crippling bouts of depression. You will deploy to Iraq and redeploy to Iraq and then volunteer to deploy to Iraq a third time to keep from facing your family, your fiancée, and reality. You will end your three-year engagement in a call center at Al Asad Air Base in western Iraq. You will sit in a chair at a cubby that reminds you of middle school. A black pay phone hangs on the back wall, and when the line goes dead you will feel as though your entire body is at a loss for feeling.

It will be a long time before sensation returns.

Self-Diagnosis:
I Want to Go Home Now

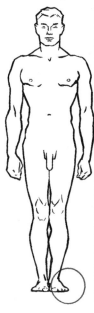

Patient suffers from ingrown toenail on fifth distal phalange, which isn't real reason for seeking medical attention. Patient needs to take a break. Is tired. Does not like being yelled at, referring to self in third person, having portholes stomped on, or anything really having to do with United States Marine Corps. Patient wants to quit as he has quit many other things in life—college, relationships, etc. Wants to quit because does not like not knowing. Or the unknown. Patient believes unknown is scary. Wants to know. Patient does not understand life is not knowing. Will be a long life.

Living in the Third Person

THIS RECRUIT IS NOT SPECIAL. He is like all other recruits. He addresses all recruits as Recruit [insert last name]. He addresses all drill instructors as Drill Instructor [insert rank and last name]. If a drill instructor is not available and this recruit needs to speak with one, he stands at arm's length from the hatch to the senior drill instructor's office; he slaps the two-inch-thick piece of raw pine nailed next to the door as hard as the nerve endings in his palm will allow, and he announces, in a loud, boisterous manner, Recruit [insert last name] requests permission to speak with Drill Instructor [insert rank and last name]. He then waits at the position of attention until the drill instructor presents himself. This recruit eats at the same time the other recruits eat, pisses when they piss, shits when they shit, runs when they run, sweats when they sweat, showers when they shower.

He lies awake in his rack at night in the position of attention, as he's been trained. He stares out the squad bay window with the other recruits and watches the lights from San Diego International Airport. He sees planes take off and land and thinks, like all the other recruits, that it would be easy to leave the squad bay late at night, sneak across the Recruit Depot, and somehow make it to the airport, where some valiant citizen might pay for a plane ticket to Canada. He thinks these thoughts until Drill Instructor [insert rank and last name] enters the squad bay and insults the recruit on duty's mother, tells the recruit on duty that Jodie—a fictional bull stud—back home is having his way with the duty recruit's girl, whom Drill Instructor [insert rank and last name] refers to as Susie Rottencrotch, and then tells him to shut off the lights.

One hundred eyelids close in unison.

When he wakes at night, his bladder straining against his receding waistline, this recruit must remember to do a set of no less than five pull-ups at the bars next to the entry of the head both before and after his business. This recruit's actions are monitored by the recruit on duty that hour and recorded in a logbook.

This recruit can still make decisions of his own. For instance, he might decide to multitask and use the shitters instead of just the urinal. The shitters do not have doors, but they have partitions, unlike most other places on the Depot. The squad bay shitters are only to be utilized at night; if this recruit or any other recruit is caught defecating in the shitters during daylight hours, the punishment is the quarterdeck.

No recruits know what happens if a recruit is caught masturbating in the shitters. Neither this recruit, nor any other recruit, has been able to get a hard-on since coming to the Depot. The imagined quarterdeck punishment makes these recruits ill and is enough to keep them limp-dicked for thirteen weeks.

This recruit tries to avoid the quarterdeck; he refuses to stare at the ten-by-twenty square of dark green linoleum. The linoleum covering the remainder of the squad bay is black. This recruit believes that the discoloration of the linoleum is not intentional. He believes the discoloration to be caused by the countless gallons of sweat, blood, vomit, tears, snot, and bile absorbed from the bodies of past recruits. This recruit wonders if dark green is the color of a soul.

On the quarterdeck Drill Instructor [insert rank and last name] commands, Push-ups, right now; side straddle hops, right now; faster, right now; mountain climbers, right now; no, push-ups, right goddamned now; steam engines, right now; faster, right now; flutter kicks, right now; side straddle hops, right goddamned now.

These recruits hear rumors. Drill instructors are not to utilize the quarterdeck for more than five minutes at a time. The drill instructors ignore this mandate. That, or quarterdeck time is slower than real time.

Later, in a desert, digging a fighting hole into the side of a hill overlooking a main supply route in one-hundred-twenty-degree heat, this recruit will come to dream of those times on the quarterdeck. He will long for them. He'll think back, and he'll wish he were there as Drill Instructor [insert rank and last name] spits wintergreen-flavored chewing tobacco into this recruit's face screaming, Faster. Faster, right now. Faster, right goddamned now.

Word of Mouth

FADE IN:

Int. Shower Room

Recruit MATTHEW MARKS *and Recruit* MATTHEW YOUNG *are cleaning Platoon 2082's shower room during Sunday field day. Marks and Young are average height and build. Marks is sinewy, with red hair (mere stubble) and milk-white skin covered in freckles. Young's own stubble is brown, and he's still working off some of the fat accrued in the year after high school, before he joined the Marines. Both are clothed in green-on-green PT gear, black athletic shoes, and white crew socks. Their faces are sunburned; their legs and arms are blocked by tan lines at mid thigh and mid bicep. They're hunched over, polishing aluminum shower trees with Brasso metal polish and sock rags. We find them in the middle of a conversation.*

13

Marks: You're getting ahead of yourself.

Young: How do you mean?

Marks: Well—do you think we just go to the fleet after this?

Young: I don't, now that you said it like that.

Marks: How do you think you get a specialty?

Young: I figured they'd sort it out in the fleet.

Marks: You got to go to the School of Infantry before you hit the fleet—you get a job there. Until then you're just 03XX.

Young: How long is that?

Marks: Two months.

Young: Fuck me. You're fucking with me, right?

Marks: Not fucking with you. Two months. I got a buddy from back home there right now, and he got stuck on a camp guard rotation. He's been there three.

Young: Three months?

Marks: That's pretty standard information.

Enter DRILL INSTRUCTOR SERGEANT ANDERSON, medium build Caucasian, runner's physique, nose like a California condor. He wears a Charlie dress uniform—green wool pants, khaki short sleeve shirt—and a Smokey Bear cover. His face is cloaked in an angry sheen of sweat.

Drill Instructor Sergeant Anderson: You Marys better be Brassoing my doggone shower trees in here and not running your fucking sucks.

Marks and Young pop to attention.

Marks and Young: Yes, sir!

Drill Instructor Sergeant Anderson: Now you're lying to me, too? Fuck no. Get on my quarterdeck right doggone now, recruits.

Marks and Young: Aye, aye, sir!

Recruits exit the shower room running toward the quarterdeck with Drill Instructor Sergeant Anderson on their heels. The thrashing commences OFF CAMERA. We can hear Drill Instructor Sergeant Anderson's commands echo around the porcelain-tiled shower room. The slaying ends. Young and Marks reenter the shower room at a run. They retrieve their rags, move to the next shower tree, and begin polishing once again. It's as if nothing has interrupted them.

Young: So, two months?

Marks: At least.

Young: My recruiter. What a cocksucker. How come you know all this shit? You're not even going infantry.

Marks: We all got to do something like it. While you're at SOI I go to Marine Combat Training at the same place—only mine's a month. Then I go to A-school.

Young: What's the *A* stand for?

Marks: I don't know.

Young: And your buddy's really been there three months?

Marks: Far as I know.

Young: Where is it?

Marks: Up north.

Young: North?

Marks: The base up north. You know, Pendleton?

Young ceases polishing and stares blankly at Marks.

Marks: Fuck me, Young. You're hopeless. Camp Pendleton is where we go for second phase. We run the Crucible there. You heard of the fucking Crucible?

Young: Yeah, asshole, I know what the fucking—

Enter Drill Instructor Sergeant Anderson. Marks sees him first and pops to attention. Young follows suit.

Drill Instructor Sergeant Anderson: All right, dick stains, you want the Crucible?

Marks and Young: No, sir!

Drill Instructor Sergeant Anderson: Too fucking bad. Quarterdeck. Now.

Marks and Young: Aye, aye, sir!

Recruits exit the shower room running toward the quarterdeck; Drill Instructor Sergeant Anderson strolls after them this time. Moments later we hear the slaying commence. Drill Instructor Sergeant Anderson's voice is too fast to discern the different exercises he directs to the two recruits. And then the slaying ends and we hear footsteps slapping down the tiled hall. Young and Marks reenter the shower room, this time out of breath. They pick up their rags and move once more to the next shower tree.

Young: Maybe we should just clean?
Marks: Think it really matters?

Crouched in the shower room, they stare at each other for a moment. The distant shouting and yelling from the cleaning happening in the squad bay and other portions of the head and the sounds of anguish from the quarterdeck are their background. They resume cleaning.

Young: So. Camp Pendleton?
Marks: Yeah we go up there for rifle qual and the Crucible.
Young: When?
Marks: Like I said, second phase. So, like, a week?
Young: I wish I would've known all this shit. You're saying it's going to be five months before I even get to the fleet? Do we go right to SOI after basic?
Marks: We get ten days of leave after all this. And you could even get recruiter's assistance if you wanted.
Young: What the fuck is that?
Marks: You're fucking hopeless.

The camera PANS UP TO Drill Instructor Sergeant Anderson standing with his arms crossed. The brim of his Smokey Bear hides his eyes and a smile graces his lips. We don't know how long he's been standing there, but we can assume quite a while.

Drill Instructor Sergeant Anderson: Fuck me, right?

Marks and Young immediately pop to attention.

Marks and Young: No, sir.
Drill Instructor Sergeant Anderson: Bullshit. Well, fuck you both. Get on my quarterdeck. Right. Fucking. Now.
Marks and Young: Aye, aye, sir!

The recruits exit at a run, slipping on the slick floor. The camera RECEDES INTO THE FAR CORNER of the shower room, PANNING the chipped white tile studded by six immaculate shower trees. Drill Instructor Sergeant Anderson, silhouetted in the opening, pivots on his heel and follows the recruits. We hear him whistling "The Marines' Hymn" down the hall. The chaos echoes off the mildewed walls and we can discern the counting of cadence and repetition from recruits on the quarterdeck over all things. A recruit runs in and turns off the light. The caterwaul dies down, and is replaced with the preparation to sleep.

All Recruits: Good night, Chesty Puller, wherever you are!
Drill Instuctor Sergeant Anderson: Prepare to sleep!

All Recruits: (Collective intake of breath.)
Drill Instructor Sergeant Anderson: Sleep!
All Recruits: (Mass exhalation.)

FADE OUT.

Seeking a Higher Power

THIS RECRUIT IS LOST. THIS recruit is lonely. This recruit has made a mistake. This recruit is not supposed to be here. This recruit misses his dog, and Steak 'n Shake patty melts, and sleeping in on Saturdays, and family, and choices, and love, and cigarettes, and his warm girlfriend, and falling asleep with his face buried in her hair, and his own hair—now mere stubble—and friends, and television, and his mother, who he's decided he's not really mad at.

Because this recruit is missing so many things, he has been given replacements. This recruit has been given physical training, and screaming from his diaphragm, and motivation through hate and fear and collective punishment, and field day, and Brasso, and hygiene, and brotherhood.

This recruit attends Mass on the first Sunday of basic training, because it is a thing that has been given.

At the front of the chapel a large retractable screen, on which the pastor/reverend/priest/chaplain—whatever he is—displays his sermon, takes up an entire wall. The chapel is air-conditioned and the pews are padded. And there are no drill instructors. This recruit loses control of his eyelids. He feels every single eyelash collide, the sound like so many cars crashing echoes through his inner ears.

Music wakes this recruit. When he wakes, everyone is standing. The pastor/reverend/priest/chaplain tells these recruits to join hands. There are blinking words on the large screen, which cease their blinking as an animated red ball begins to bounce across their jagged stark peaks, and the chapel—now more a revival tent—is filled with voices. This recruit scans the room and watches tears stream from eyeballs and snot bubbles pop from nostrils. Recruits begin to sway and the recruits on either side of this recruit tighten their grips, and this recruit can hear their voices grow taut like overtightened guitar strings. This recruit reciprocates their hand squeezing and begins to sing in tune and in time with the music and words on the screen. By the time the ball has bounced itself out and the pastor/reverend/priest/chaplain asks these recruits to please be seated this recruit is all in. His mother attends and works in a church, though he has never been interested. He thinks maybe this could be a way to heal that relationship, to have a piece of home, to experience love in this hard place.

This recruit has found religion.

But this recruit marches to the chapel and follows the bouncing ball's directions and laughs at the pastor/reverend/priest/chaplain's bad jokes only one more Sunday. That second Sunday night, when the recruit lay leader asks this recruit to lead the group in prayer this recruit stutters because he does not know any prayers. When the lay leader asks about his church's denomination back home this recruit becomes flustered and cannot answer because he does not know what denomination his mother is. The recruit lay leader looks at this recruit like people look at ugly dogs in animal shelters. This recruit begins to speak, to explain himself, but another recruit speaks over him. This recruit feels like a tourist. He will cease to attend prayers and services on Sundays, and will instead stay behind to clean the head, read the newspaper, and write letters to his girlfriend, whom his drill instructors refer to as Susie Rottencrotch.

In his rack the night after his last Sunday service and lay leader meeting, he thinks of the hand-holding and the swaying and the red bouncing ball and how it told him when to sing, and how the lay leader looked at him with expectance and then pity. This recruit feels his face grow hot with disgust and shame at his longing for the comfort of his mother—of his past life. He resolves to be harder. To take the grief, sadness, and despair brought on by loss and perform alchemy on those emotions, to turn them into determination, anger, and strength. Like anything in the Marine Corps, if this recruit does it and thinks it and performs it enough, it will become automatic, ingrained in the muscle forever. It will become truth.

Prepare to Eat

AT CAMP PENDLETON IN MAY 2005, in between Crucible obstacle stations, an orange is placed in this recruit's hand. No one has told this recruit what to do with the orange and so he does nothing. But he is anxious about the orange. How will he eat the orange correctly if no one tells him how?

Hasn't he eaten countless different fruits in his lifetime? This recruit may have once peeled an apple in one long glossy strand, sliced it into sections, dipped it in honey or peanut butter. Afterward, he might have ground the peel and core in the garbage disposal and washed the small particulate matter down the city wastewater pipe.

Where did that apple come from? Did this recruit's mother or father buy it from a grocery store? Does this recruit even have a mother? Did this recruit pick it off a tree in his backyard? Did he ever have a backyard? This recruit does not remember being issued any of these things.

This recruit must not have been in formation when he ate the fruit. This recruit must not have been in a desert when he ate the fruit. He must not have had a past-its-prime rucksack strapped to his shoulders, the framework wearing through the kidney pad, metal digging into the small of his back, breaking open freshly scabbed skin. This recruit's face must not have been covered in camouflage grease paint and he could not have known words like portholes or inkstick or gofasters or quarter-deck. Was there a time like that?

Weren't there times this recruit cut up bananas and put the pieces in pancake batter that sizzled and popped on a griddle covered in melted butter? Weren't there times when he sliced an orange in half and juiced it? What would he have done with the rind?

This recruit stands in formation with the weight of the orange in his left palm. He thinks of how he could measure its roundness. A laser micrometer maybe. How does this recruit know that term? No drill instructor has ever said that term. What was before this?

Ears.

Open, sir.

Fuck no, ears.

Open, sir.

No trash, good to go?

This recruit hears the commands through his thoughts.

Don't leave any doggone trash. Nothing. Not one doggone thing goes in your cargo pockets. Recruits don't put anything in their cargo pockets. Cargo pockets do not exist. Recruits for all intents and purposes do not know the meaning of cargo pockets. Good to go?

Yes, sir.

Sit down, right now.

Aye, aye, sir.

Prepare to eat.

Aye, aye, sir.

Eat, right now.

Aye, aye, sir.

Now this recruit is left in the dirt, and all around him, recruits are biting into their fruit. He sees another recruit try to place a banana peel in his cargo pocket, which isn't supposed to exist. A drill instructor pulls the banana-peel recruit out of formation and runs screaming behind him to a place this recruit cannot see and does not wish to.

This recruit is alone with his orange. It rests in the palm of his hand, a miniature desert sun. This recruit imagines the juice in his mouth, sliding down his throat, lighting up his insides. With the orange at his lips, this recruit unhinges his mandible like a snake swallowing an egg. The orange's flesh is thick. Microvesicles full of citric acid pop as his jaw closes, his skin tingling. Everything burns, tongue, gums, throat, face, lips. The juice double-times down his chin, pools into his cupped hands, and he forgets that there might have been another way to eat a piece of fruit. This is, has been, and will be, the only way. Ever.

Targets Appear

SIX WEEKS INTO BASIC TRAINING, in the prone shooting position, this recruit slips the butt stock of his rifle into the pocket of his shoulder and draws a bead on a dog target. This is what he sees:

Not a dog, but a human.

One day, when this recruit is no longer this recruit he will wonder if this was purposeful, if it was meant to dehumanize the target, if it was a cosmic joke, or just a coincidence of Marine Corps nomenclature.

But not right now.

Right now this recruit wonders what it will be like to load live 5.56mm ball rounds into his magazines, to slide the curvaceous thirty-round-capacity aluminum case into the magazine well until the catch pops like a pussy. He imagines the feeling of sight alignment, sight picture, breathing, exhaling, squeezing the trigger, watching the shot find its home.

During classroom instruction at Camp Pendleton, this recruit sits on aluminum bleachers for hours learning about the fundamentals of marksmanship from a primary marksmanship instructor who crams his trigger finger in his nostril to the second knuckle, inspects his find, and wipes the aftermath on his utilities.

After classroom instruction, this recruit takes his rifle and circles with other recruits in sandy crabgrass around white fifty-five-gallon drums covered in spray-painted stencils of the three target types—Able, Dog, B-Modified—while the PMI demonstrates how to make loop slings, which cinch high around nonfiring biceps and wrap nonfiring forearms, and choke blood flow, but also increase firing stability.

The PMI walks the circles of recruits and expounds on the necessity of stock weld—what he calls chipmunk cheek. He sells proper eye relief like snake oil, joins rifle butts into shoulder pockets and preaches high firm pistol grips. He uses phrases like skeletal support and bone-to-meat contact. The rifle he holds seems to have sprouted from his hand: an extra appendage. The PMI takes this recruit's glasses, affectionately called birth control goggles, and uses athletic tape to attach a foam earplug to the inside of the nosepiece while explaining that it will help this recruit achieve proper eye relief.

This recruit learns the prone position is the most stable firing platform, then sitting, then kneeling, then standing. The PMI rotates recruits through positions, an hour in the kneeling, in the standing, in the sitting. He focuses least on the prone.

This recruit hears the racking of other recruits' M16A2 lightweight, magazine-fed, gas-operated, air-cooled, shoulder-fired rifle charging handles, the click of ejection port covers, and crisp snaps of hammers slamming into the head ends of firing pins. In his rack that night the sounds echo in his ears like church bells.

This recruit has never shot a gun. He wants to know what it will feel like when the round casing ejects from the side of his rifle and the bullet explodes from the muzzle. He learns about parabolic flight, how gravity acts on a bullet from the very moment it is fired, dragging it to the earth. He learns about elevation and windage and how to adjust his front sight post when achieving a battlesight zero.

He wants to know what it will feel like when the targets are people. He wants to know what it is like to be shot at and return fire. He wants to believe it is all as easy as WMD and jihad and democracy-in-danger. He wants to kill some raghead terrorist motherfuckers. He wants to tell his family at home that war is hell and he wants to give the thousand-yard stare when he says it. He wants people to ask him what it's like to kill and he wants to be able to tell them. He wants to be feared. He wants to deploy to war this very second. He wants to go home. He wants to be a hero. He wants to go back in time and go to college, to a time before nomenclatures and acronyms and Susie Rotten-crotch this and faggot that and drill here and quarterdeck there. He wants to rip the tape and earplug from his goddamn glasses. He wants. Every time he holds the rifle he wants and wants and wants and in his mind he sights in on each and every single want and gives a slow, steady squeeze with his death-dealing trigger finger as he reaches the valley of his breathing rhythm. He blows them away.

The Drill Instructor at Rest

IT IS JUNE 2005, THE last days of third phase. The recruit company is back in San Diego from Camp Pendleton. The drill instructor stands at the entrance of the barracks shower room and shouts commands at the recruits.

Soap! Place that doggone bar of soap in your right hand and lather your left arm. Now take that doggone bar of soap and place it in your left hand and lather your right arm.

He names various parts of the recruits' bodies and has them fill in the blank canvas with soap bubbles like a paint-by-numbers. This used to amuse him. At one time he thought the cheap broken shower shoes flopping around the recruits' ankles were a poignant metaphor for something, but he no longer remembers what. His time at the Depot is drawing near an end. He's a heavy hat, a second in command, has never been a senior drill instructor, thinks maybe he won't ever be.

Make sure you get your nasty damn heads. Every recruit, right now, rub that doggone soap on your grape.

He's tired. So goddamned tired.

It's the last night of the cycle and still these nasty fucks have to be showered by the numbers.

He knows full well if he doesn't walk them through it Barney-style they'll curl their grimy asses up on the floor, use the towels as pillows, and take a nap.

In his mind he rambles off the creed he's recited more times than he's said I love you to his mother: These recruits are entrusted to my care. I will train them to the best of my ability. I will develop them into smartly disciplined, physically fit, basically-trained Marines, thoroughly indoctrinated in love of Corps and Country. I will demand of them, and demonstrate by my own example, the highest standards of personal conduct, morality, and professional skill.

Then he thinks, Fuck these recruits. If I don't kill one of them, it'll be a good day. If I can get just one of them to know their ass from their elbow, I will die happy. However, I will confuse the hell out of them until they don't know up from down. Also, I vow to never let them catch me napping in the DI lounge.

The soapy mess of bodies in front of him whimpering from stinging eyes graduates tomorrow. Today he had to hand them their Eagle, Globe, and Anchor emblems and call them Marines. The drill instructor grimaces and holds down his gorge.

Gonzalez (whom he calls Gorditas) blubbered all over himself. Young wasn't wearing his goddamn BCGs. He knows he told that motherfucker he wasn't to wear the contacts his family sent until graduation. Then again, Young couldn't even get the handshake and acceptance of the pin right—maybe the motherfucker just hadn't worn anything and couldn't see. And goddamn Duffy (whom he calls Doofus)—somehow Doofus's fat fucking belly has gotten fatter.

All right fuck stains, turn on those doggone shower trees and rinse your nasty fucking bodies so you get all clean and pretty for Susie-fucking-Rottencrotch tomorrow. Then towel the fuck off and get changed over for hygiene inspection—and send me five recruits to come clean the Whiskey Locker by twenty-one hundred. That's fifteen mikes, ladies.

Recruit Kelley requests permission to speak with the drill instructor, sir.

What, numbnuts?

This recruit and other recruits are wondering if these recruits who are PFCs should place their rank on their cammies for tomorrow morning's chow, sir.

The drill instructor squinches his face together and parrots Kelley. Though Kelley looks so ridiculous at the position of attention, small olive drab shower towel over his dick, that to keep from laughing the drill instructor lowers his Smokey Bear over his face and gives a quick yes.

The drill instructor performs a perfect about-face, steps, right faces into a walk down the hall past the head, left faces into the squad bay, continues for a few steps, and left faces once more through the hatch to the drill instructor's office, slapping the pine as he does so and saying to himself as he enters, Bad motherfucker on deck, sir.

In the office the drill instructor breathes asbestos insulation and recruit body odor. He has the squad bay solo tonight. He knows those goddamn Marys are chattering in the shower room, talking about the pussy they're going to get and beer they're going to drink. He hates them. Every last goddamned one. He knows there must've been a time when he felt proud to graduate a platoon. When did that change? This job is killing him. His back aches and his feet hurt. He is on the go damn near twenty-four-seven for thirteen weeks at a stretch.

Maybe it *is* just time to go, he thinks. But when he leaves, what will the fleet have for him? In the fleet he'll return to accounting. He doesn't think he can hack disbursing checks in a tiny shitcan office on Pendleton or Lejeune—or worse, the Stumps.

He'd loved this once—making Marines. He wants badly to love it again.

Recruits file past his open door, not turning their backs, looking through the hatch and smiling. One of them waves and before he can stop himself the drill instructor waves back.

And then a funny thing happens.

The drill instructor's insides expand, and implode. He supernovas, and collapses into a black hole. He is out the hatch and into the squad bay, a dervish of screaming and cursing and drill instructor speak only recruits understand. He rotates them in shifts of ten to the quarterdeck—side straddle hops, mountain climbers, star jumps, high knees, hello Dollys, flutter kicks, push-ups, steam engines—while the rest of the platoon waits in the push-up position grunting and breathing heavily. He flips racks and dumps footlockers and spits in the new Marines' faces as their bodies sweat and collapse on the quarterdeck.

The drill instructor's love rises like a phoenix. Except instead of ashes it births itself slimy and gruesome from hate and pain and fanatical devotion to the Corps, and as the recruits huff and grow red-faced and lose their guts over the quarterdeck he feels their hate, their love, and he becomes Death, the destroyer of worlds.

The next day as he poses for photos with the new Marines and their parents, and then watches them walk to rental cars and taxis, the drill instructor's face contorts into a smile he doesn't tip his hat to hide.

Self-Diagnosis: Ouch

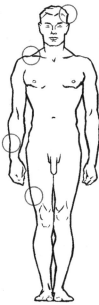

Patient suffered a physical incident. Concussive injury to brain, sprain to right shoulder, lacerations to right arm, lacerations and contusion to right thigh. These things not concern of patient. Patient suffers from existential crisis. Wondering the point. Will concussion matter? Will injuries and deaths of other Marines matter? The hours of lost sleep and the lost minds and scars and the collateral damage. Patient wants to know if any of it will matter. Advise patient: two days light duty, change socks, take Motrin, turn off brain.

Legend

IN THE SUMMER OF 2005 at the School of Infantry on Camp Pendleton we are separated by specialty: machine gunners, mortarmen, assaultmen, TOW gunners, infantrymen.

Some of us take a qualification indoctrination to become reconnaissance men. Most of us fail.

We cannot hold a rifle above our heads and tread water and we are afraid to take the water into our lungs to accomplish our given task, and so we fail because we will not try.

Those who pass the indoc must become basic infantrymen in order to go on to basic reconnaissance school.

The rest of us have a choice.

Chris Smith and Randy Lawson are hulks. They choose to be machine gunners. Chris is half-Filipino and smiles big white Chiclets when he talks about his father, an M60 gunner in Vietnam.

Randy is ethnically ambiguous. Growing up, his hero was Jean-Claude Van Damme. Randy can do the splits in a doorway; he demonstrates this and we are amazed.

Fernando Vargas, whose family comes from Rosarito, Mexico, chooses TOW gunner. He wants to fire tube-launched, optically-tracked, wire-guided missiles. TOW gunners and assaultmen blend together and cross-train because there aren't enough volunteers.

The mortarmen are lazy doughy white boys like Andrew Laughlin, a Private Pyle lookalike, but who is too meek to crack and become homicidal. There is also Ned Lewis, who is black and has arms like the steel mortar tubes he carries on hikes.

The infantrymen are called grunts and crunchies. They are stupid and intelligent and cruel and beautiful and black and white and brown and yellow and fat and lazy and lithe and godlike and frightening in their dedication to death.

We become grunts. We want to be basic, jacks-of-all-trades and masters of none, meat for the grinder. We want to pay for what we think might be the sins accrued in our hard lives by the time we are nineteen through violent death and become tragic heroes that other SOI instructors tell stories about in hushed tones.

Our instructors are like drill instructors if drill instructors weren't like hermetically sealed action figures. The SOI instructors are gritty and lean, with hollow eyes and acid wit. In garrison they fidget and stress and fuck with our time, make us clean, make us run, make us hurt. In the field the instructors loosen;

they tell us war stories about Fallujah and Ramadi and Mosul and Nasiriyah, about climbing six-foot-high mud walls in full gear while baking in one-hundred-degree heat and taking enemy fire. In the stories there is always death, there is always loss. We sit on our packs in the coastal hills that smell like hot dirt and the sweat of the hundreds of thousands of Marines who came before us and we keep our faces solemn. We can never meet our instructors' eyes so we stare at our boots instead.

From us the instructors demand perfection and endurance and fortitude and leadership and an inhuman ability to stay awake. They expect us to see in the dark, to anticipate the movement of our enemy, to act as magnanimous killing machines.

Still, they fuck with us in the field. They make us run in flak jackets with our rifles. They make us perform eight-count bodybuilders until we vomit our MREs in the dust. They make us run full speed, screaming war cries until our throats bleed. If we do not seek cover in the dirt fast enough, they tell us we are dead and our squad mates must pull our bodies to a casualty collection point and we run the range again and again— thousands of meters—until we get it right.

The instructors bless some of us with squad leader billets. We are in charge of our peers in the field. We lead them and ensure they are prepared and try to be hard like our instructors. When our peers fail it is not their fault, it is ours. When we fall asleep in our fighting holes and neglect to wake our squad for a mission brief one of our instructors football punts our helmets and relieves us of command. Deep down we are relieved; we think maybe now we get to tell our own stories, that they won't end in death. We are so young.

When we all graduate and are sent to Third Battalion, Fifth Marine Regiment at Camp San Mateo at the north end of Camp Pendleton, the machine gunners and other heavy weapons are sent to Weapons Company or are doled out to heavy weapons platoons in one of the line companies—India, Lima, or Kilo. We are expecting one of those three. But the needs of the Corps take precedence in the fleet and while we watch our fellow grunts receive their line assignments we are sent to Weapons Company where we'll be made into mortarmen—tube strokers, gun bunnies. Everything we tried to avoid. We understand now; choice is an illusion. It is a good lesson to learn.

Special Features

THIS IS ME, IN THE present. I'm looking back at a movie of me in the past—Past-me. I'll play you some of the movie and you can look at me, too.

Allow me to commentate.

The backstory: suburban childhood, chubby kid who got picked on, broken home, drugs and drinking, poor choices, shitty jobs, mounds of self-loathing, the decision to make a change, basic training, etc., etc. In light of all that, let's skip to the chapter titled "A Bad Joke."

Watch and listen as School of Infantry instructor Sergeant Johnson tells Past-me and his class in late summer of 2005 they'll be stationed at a unit in Hawaii and that their unit will be heading off to Australia and Okinawa and Thailand and other beautiful places. Past-me thinks this sounds fantastic. Past-me was scared and now isn't, because there are no wars in those places that concern him. Only beautiful scenery and women and beaches and drinks with little umbrellas.

Move on to the next scene weeks later where Sergeant Johnson informs Past-me and his class that he has lied and they'll instead be moving just down the road to Third Battalion, Fifth Marine Regiment at Camp San Mateo, a unit that returned from Iraq in April 2005 and will be heading back in January 2006.

Now, if we slow it down a bit—there! Just there, did you catch it? The fear in Past-me's eyes, the color draining from his sunburnt face, the muscles of his jaw clenching, grinding teeth to powder. That's the reaction to the pit forming in Past-me's stomach. Follow the camera as it pans to Past-me's point of view. We can see Sergeant Johnson in slow motion. Watch his dead shark eyes begin to teem with life and the barest hint of a smirk stretch over the wad of dip tucked into his lower lip. Sergeant Johnson is pleased. He is a combat veteran, a hard man, still young, maybe twenty-five. He knows the horror and fear and mind-numbing boredom of war. He misses those things—just as Past-me will come to miss them—and making Past-me and his training class feel frightened is a way he can experience a small slice of that pleasure. Past-me does not yet understand these complexities. In this moment, Past-me only wants to cover himself with blankets, clutch his stuffed dog, stick his thumb in his mouth, and forget about the world.

Past-me does not do this.

Instead, Past-me weeps on the pier in Oceanside, and weeps in the designated smoke pit outside the PX after graduating from the School of Infantry, and weeps in the lavatory on the plane to Iraq a few chapters in the future. In fact, there is a compilation section in the special features of this DVD devoted entirely to scenes containing Past-me weeping.

Skip to the DVD chapter titled "Go Fuck Yourself, Young."

Notice Past-me's interactions with senior Marines after being assigned to Third Battalion, Fifth Marine Regiment in September 2005:

Hey, Young! Get over here.

Watch as Private First Class Past-me jogs up to the senior Marine without answering because he can't remember the corporal's name.

I guess I don't rate a greeting? Fuck me, right? I guess we don't sound off, either. Know what happens to boots who don't sound off, boot?

No, Corporal.

They get fucking dead, Young. You want to fucking die, boot?

No, Corporal.

Too fucking bad, because you're going to fucking get your head blown off over there because you don't have the fucking stones to sound off and no one will know where you are and you'll just run into a building and some other Marine's going to think you're a fucking hajji and shoot you right in your stupid fucking face.

Yes, Corporal.

Get the fuck out of here, Young.

Aye, aye, Corporal.

Past-me is often told he will die. He is told he will die because he hasn't cleaned his barracks room properly. He is told because he lacks attention to detail he will be shot in the face. He is told he will not only get himself killed, but that he'll get his friends killed as well. Past-me is told he will die so often that at times he wonders maybe if he isn't dead already.

This next DVD chapter, "If You're Scared, Go to Church," takes place in January 2006 before Past-me and his company are to load the buses that will carry us to March Air Force Base, where they will board the plane that will fly them to war. See all the families of junior Marines walking around the barracks? Past-me's family didn't come. Past-me told them not to. Most of those families are from the surrounding Southern California area. They're spending some last precious moments with their sons before sending them off to fight in a conflict they probably don't support.

Watch the barracks staircase. In about five seconds, a Marine—Sergeant Carmichael—is going to descend those stairs. He is short and barrel-chested and tattooed, with thinning red hair and a West Virginia accent. But you don't need that information to know who he is. Simply look for the Marine screaming, If you're scared, go to church. No one is quite sure what this phrase means, but it sounds intimidating.

Sergeant Carmichael also screams, We are going to die. He tells Past-me and his comrades they are going to lose their legs, and their brothers are going to bleed out in their arms. Sergeant

Carmichael tells the junior Marines he does not trust a single one of them and that they are going to get him killed, too.

Sergeant Carmichael forces Marines to the position of attention in front of their families and makes them tell their parents goodbye forever. He says, Tell them you love them. Tell them you're sorry. He screams until Past-me's squad leader, Sergeant Mars, escorts him out of sight to a barracks room.

Past-me knows Sergeant Carmichael has not yet deployed to combat and that he is afraid, just as Past-me is afraid. Past-me also knows Sergeant Carmichael is drunk, and Past-me wishes to be drunk as well. Past-me relishes the thought of losing his inhibitions and exclaiming to the world, I am going to die.

Past-me recognizes that this feeling, this need to exclaim and acknowledge, is how Sergeant Johnson, the School of Infantry instructor, once felt when he also thought he would die in war and how every other man who has ever gone to war has felt.

Watch as I fast-forward through all of what comes next. Watch Past-me become what Sergeant Johnson became. Watch Past-me not die and wish he had. Watch Past-me struggle to live for something just as Sergeant Johnson once did. In 16x speed, watch Past-me haze new joins and bar fight his knuckles to shreds and cheat on his fiancée and volunteer to redeploy and drive drunk and burn bridges and hate everyone and himself—just to try to get back to that feeling of exhilaration at the thought of dying.

Watch me.

45

How to Make a Portable Partner
(Patent Pending)

HEY THERE, DEVIL DOGS. ARE you feeling lonely? Are you currently training in the field—away from everything you know and love? Have you been awake for more than thirty-six hours? Has it been more than three months since you've seen or even spoken to a woman? Are you sick of chafing the sensitive skin of your nethers against callused, sand-covered hands? Well, have I got news for you.

Thanks to Staff Sergeant Rick Footman's easy-to-use-and-transport Portable Partner (patent pending), you'll never go without pussy again. Now, I know what you're thinking, but this isn't like other portable masturbatory devices; it's a system all its own, designed for maximum comfort and portability.

Never again will a faux flesh hole cluttering up your kit embarrass you. Never again will you have to wash your own (or, dare I say, someone else's) spunk from hard-to-reach nooks and crannies. Never again will you experience the chagrin of losing or forgetting your expensive-brand pocket pussy—now that there's the Portable Partner (patent pending).

Other systems can cost fifty, sixty, even seventy dollars, while the Portable Partner (patent pending) is *free*. That's right, *free*. All you need to do is put those grunt skills to work and beg, borrow, or steal.

The story of Portable Partner (patent pending) and its creator, Rick Footman, exists alongside stories of Nikola Tesla and Gary Kildall, and all those inventors who have endeavored to increase the quality of life for their fellow human beings.

The month was November of the year 2005, just before my first pump over to the sandbox during a joint training exercise. It was in the back of a Humvee: Rick revealed to me the genius of his invention as we bumped across the Mojave, tank engines screaming next to our vehicle, five-hundred-pounders dropping from fast movers overhead. Rick sat toward the cab of the Humvee, his slender Western lawman frame angled and sharp. The chinstrap of his Kevlar hung below his rectangular dimpled chin; mirrored sunglasses kept his visage blank aside from a widening grin spreading across his tanned, smooth cheeks. He noticed my enamored gaze and became serious.

Young, would you take a look at something for me? he asked.

Sure, Staff Sergeant, I said.

The others in the back of the Humvee were silent; they spit tobacco and bumped around on wooden bench seats, sweat pooled at their throat protectors.

Without warning Staff Sergeant Footman flipped the tan triangle of his groin protector into the air, revealing his testicles.

See any silver in there, Young? He slapped the flaccid exposed flesh. My wife keeps complaining about gray hairs.

Staff Sergeant, someone said. What's wrong with your balls? They're huge.

And then, fellas, then Rick revealed his secret. Pay close attention.

I'll tell you, he said. I haven't jerked off the entire month we've been here, but I'm really going to treat myself when we finish up tonight.

You got a Fleshlight, Staff Sergeant? I asked.

Fuck no, that shit's expensive. I make my own.

And there it is, gents. That's how I learned Rick's secret. The secret I'll share here with you today so you won't find yourself paying upward of fifty, sixty, even seventy dollars to get your rocks off, the secret of the Portable Partner (patent pending).

First things first, you'll need some miscellaneous items to build your own Portable Partner (patent pending). Keep in mind, these items can most likely be found for free on any camp, forward operating base, observation post, or patrol base. They can be purchased as well, but what's the point? Marines make do. We overcome; we improvise; we adapt. No door? Circle charge. No weights? Tent poles and sand bags. No pussy? Portable Partner (patent pending).

All right, now beg, borrow, or steal: one hand towel (bigger than a washcloth, smaller than a body towel), two to three heavy-gauge rubber bands, one latex or other synthetic medical glove. Last, some kind of lubricant.

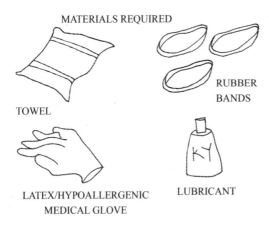

MATERIALS REQUIRED

TOWEL

RUBBER BANDS

LATEX/HYPOALLERGENIC MEDICAL GLOVE

LUBRICANT

Now we're ready to begin assembly. You're going to want to fold the towel length-wise, like so, to a width of about seven inches.

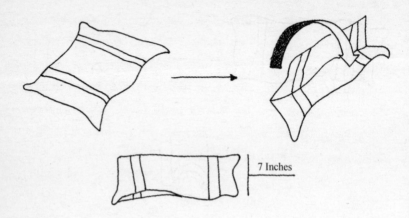

7 Inches

Take your glove and place it on left side of the towel. Fold four of the latex fingers down to the palm of the glove in order to create a single tubelike structure.

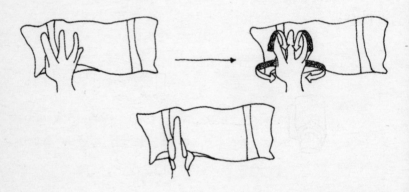

Next, roll your towel around the glove to the necessary tightness. We don't judge here, folks; not all men are created equal.

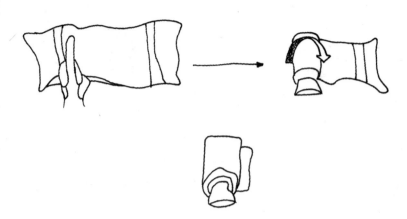

This step might be a bit complicated for you knuckle-draggers out there, so pay close attention. Secure rubber bands 1 and 2 before folding the cuff of the latex glove over the end of the rolled towel. Then, use rubber band 3 to secure the cuff in place.

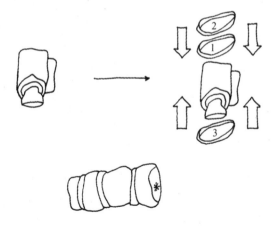

Last, holding the device vertically, insert the tip of the lubricant bottle into the opening of the device. Coat as desired. Now of course this step is completely up to you, friends. To each his own, I say.

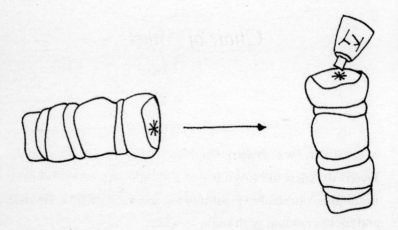

And there you have it, the Portable Partner (patent pending).

Stay awake on post, pass the time, relieve some tension, prolong your life, guard against prostate cancer. It's the affordable, single-use, do-it-yourself pocket pussy. The Portable Partner (patent pending): so you're not the only thing getting fucked on deployment.

Choir of Angels

A MEMORY: WE STAND ON line in the middle of Mojave Desert darkness in November of 2005 spotlighted by Humvee headlights, our shadows casting long and twig thin on the sand and rocks crawling with night animals.

Our seniors stand in bristled silence, sucking on cigarettes, glowing cherries the red eyes of predators. Even farther beyond our spotlight is Amboy Crater—Old Amboy—towering black sand against a black sky. Our seniors tell us it's where Lucifer landed after his fall from heaven. They tell us it's where Charles Manson raped and murdered babies.

We stand at the position of attention, our bare pale legs covered in folliculitis. I imagine our infected flesh bloating and sloughing from our bodies—bodies shivering and swaying from exhaustion as the dome of space lowers over us, sucking heat from scrub, mortar tubes left on the gun line, our bone marrow.

I am thinking I might die of hypothermia, or that we'll all be beaten to death. Maybe the freshest of us, big black Cedric Brown, who smiles more than anyone I know and has the motivation of ten men, or Charlie Beaston, whose disarming Oklahoma drawl has made us forget his newness, are not thinking this, but the rest of us know of what our salts are capable—we have seen their Handycam movies from Fallujah of bloated, bullet-riddled corpses and burning buildings. We remember their cheery, teenage voices tossing frag grenades down staircases and explaining the various fluids leaking from exit wounds. I imagine they'll drive our beaten and crippled bodies out to Old Amboy, dump us down the hollow. They'd sleep like babies.

In the outer dark, a moonbeam bobs along the gun line: Private First Class Smalley. Short and slow, with thick glasses digging in on the ridge of his too-big, cratered nose—hundreds of Old Amboys. Behind Smalley's lenses his eyes are sleepy and crossed. He stuffs his gums with Kodiak wintergreen and the shavings stick in the crevasses of his teeth and chapped lips.

Smalley, a voice from the outer dark calls.

Yes, Corporal?

Your boys are going to stand out here all fucking night, Smalley.

Yes, Corporal.

Unless you shit me those fucking aiming stakes.

Without aiming stakes we cannot fire our mortars. We cannot get the gun up. We cannot hang a round down the tube, fingers wrapped around the football shaped fuse, knuckles clenched white. We won't be able to revel in the gut-shuddering blast or the delayed splash of impact.

Adam Flynn, my mortar team's assistant gunner, seethes next to me. Smalley is our ammo man. They are our stakes that have been lost. We know it is our fault for not policing Smalley. Now everyone will be punished.

Tomorrow is the last day of mortar fire before our obsolete mortar platoon integrates with the Combined Anti-Armor Teams to form Mobile Assault Platoons. Before we have to again learn some new tactic of fighting. Adam and I want to remember the thing we have come to love fondly. We do not want to spend the shoot being hazed.

Smalley's light continues its trek, pausing at each mortar position to count the aiming stakes in the carrier bags.

And you, motherfuckers.

Yes, Corporal, we sound off in unison.

What are we going to do with you?

Sing us a lullaby, calls Vick Miner, one of our sergeants. He walks into the wedge of light, boots crunching along the dried bed of primordial ocean.

We stand, silent, at the position of attention. One of us begins "Rock-a-bye Baby."

Shut the fuck up, shit stain. Sergeant Miner's snaggled lakeweed teeth slur his words.

The crackle of cigarettes, the nocturnal desert things slithering and scampering along the hardpan, our hearts firing pins against primers.

Sing me "The Marines' Hymn," says Sergeant Miner. He holds his arms like a conductor.

Sergeant Miner's arms drop and we launch the song from our guts, mortar rounds bursting past blast attenuators, pushing air from our diaphragms, our shoulders back, chins up, eyes level. Our voices make the six feet three inches of Sergeant Miner look childish, and for the three minutes it takes to sing "The Marines' Hymn" we are a choir of angels in the darkness, spotlighted by holy Humvee high beams.

Old Amboy shrinks from our fervor as we recount the Battle of Chapultepec and the many deaths of the Barbary pirates. We've killed more than you ever will, we tell Old Amboy.

And then we are done and the stakes are found and we are in our sleeping bags, shielded by bivvy sacks against the chilly desert night, trying to imagine what war will be like. Somewhere under the starlight our voices are still zooming through the thin desert air, moving along the cooling sand and yuccas, flowing over the Mojave mountains, beyond the sadistic reach of our senior Marines, past the sacrifices at Old Amboy.

We drift into sleep waiting for the splash.

Love Story

I love you, says the boy.

I love you, too, says the girl.

Will you marry me? asks the boy.

Yes, says the girl.

This is not her first mistake.

When should we get married? asks the girl.

Why don't you come back to California with me and we'll drive to Las Vegas, says the boy. One day when we have children we'll tell them our story. We'll say, When we were young your father was shipping off to war and we were in love and so we drove to Las Vegas and got married.

The girl thinks that the boy's impulsivity is romantic. It makes her feel wanted.

Do you think there will ever be other women? asks the girl.

Of course not, says the boy. I mean, unless maybe something horrible happens, like, what if you get sick? Or die. Or, I mean, sometimes marriage just doesn't work out.

That would be a story to tell our children, says the girl.

The girl wonders if there have been other women already. The boy is handsome and he is broken by his parents' dissolved marriage and his skewed sense of manhood. It's a formula to attract naïve girls. It attracted her. It is blood in the water—sensitive and damaged but strong and protective.

Have there been other women? asks the girl.

What do you mean? asks the boy. Like, before you?

No, says the girl.

You mean since you, then? asks the boy.

Yes, says the girl.

Of course not, says the boy. I mean, there were women before you, but I'm with you now. I don't think about them.

You still talk to your ex, says the girl. You almost followed another ex to Arizona when she moved there for college, says the girl. When the boy flushes and turns his head she knows she stepped over one of his lines. The lines are fluid and twisty so usually she is over one before she knows it.

The boy does not respond.

The boy can be mean when he puts his mind to it. He burns bridges with people at the drop of a hat. Sometimes if the girl says or does something he does not like he will not speak to her, refuses to acknowledge her existence until the girl apologizes for, what seems to her, being alive.

I'm sorry, says the girl. It's just that I love you.

I love you, too, says the boy. I don't know why we can't forget that happened.

It was only a year ago, says the girl.

It was a year ago, says the boy.

Can you promise me there won't be another woman? asks the girl.

I think I want to promise that, says the boy. But don't promises just seem like if you make them, they get broken?

I promise you there won't be other men, says the girl.

But you don't need to, says the boy. Because we're in love, and love is kind of a promise, isn't it?

You just said promises are made to be broken, says the girl.

Well, says the boy. Yes. But spoken promises. Just because you say I love you doesn't mean you're making a promise. Love is more like a feeling. Like, you know I love you even if I don't talk to you for a few days, or we don't have foreplay and go to sleep right after sex, or I don't like your parents, or think your opinions are wrong. You know I love you even when I don't tell you.

The girl knows this is not a two-way street. This is how the boy is allowed to express himself. This is how he's allowed to treat her. She must be dutiful, and loving, and doting, and under-standing. She must not criticize him because he is already broken from being adopted and his adoptive parents' divorce and his father's callousness and his mother's victimhood—her criticism would not be fair because of that fact. But the boy says he loves her, and he makes her laugh sometimes, and they spend time together, and she's broken herself from her own parents' nuclear explosion of a marriage and her mother's remarrying to a suicidal Gulf War veteran and her father's remarrying to a Southern belle beauty queen who thinks the girl's curly hair makes her look poor and dirty.

Marriage is a promise, says the girl.

You're going to look beautiful in a wedding dress, says the boy. Will you send me pictures when I'm gone?

The boy asks for pictures often. Sometimes he wants pictures of the girl doing things she feels humiliated by, but still she takes them and sends them and listens to the boy talk about her body and how she should position it the next time he asks for pictures.

If you promise not to show anyone, says the girl.

Other guys show me pictures of their girlfriends, says the boy. They all think you're gorgeous. What's wrong with bragging?

I would never show pictures of you to someone else, says the girl.

I might die, says the boy. What if I died?

I don't want to talk about it, says the girl.

It always comes to death with the boy; there is no equality next to the possibility of death. The girl is not going to war. The girl is finishing high school and the girl is going to college and the girl is going to major in biology and maybe go to medical school. She feels safe most of the time, as safe as a girl can feel. She feels guilty for this, then wonders what's wrong with feeling safe. She wonders if her safety entitles the boy. She wonders if she does love the boy or if maybe it is all just guilt.

I love you, says the boy.

Deserter

IN JANUARY 2006 I'M ASLEEP in my barracks room at Camp San Mateo on the larger Camp Pendleton and almost miss my bus to war. A Marine I won't remember the name of in ten years finds me and we sprint the half mile from the barracks to the parade deck. The Marine sucks in hard and breathes out, Fuck man. Fuck. For the entire three minutes.

I think because of this, my seniors will call me a coward and a deserter and they will throw me from the charter bus as it speeds down a Southern California highway. They will stick me on point and give me the radio and send me to clear houses as first man in the stack with a squad automatic weapon, which will inevitably jam and I'll be mowed down by muj.

I wish the Marine wouldn't have found me. I wish I could've stayed asleep for the next three years only to wake for my end of active service and reenter the civilian world without the scars and trauma my seniors seem so willing to pass down.

There is an empty seat in front of Corporal MacReady—the lead vehicle commander in my platoon.

I sit next to Keene Sherburne who says, Nice going.

I am about to tell him to fuck off when Corporal MacReady leans forward and whispers in my ear, Mother. Fucker. You trying to desert?

No, Corporal, I whisper back.

Don't whisper to me, boot. I look like your fucking Susie?

No, Corporal.

This ain't a way to start a deployment, Young. This is some bad juju. Shit goes south, it's on you.

Corporal MacReady leans back and closes his eyes. He's snoring before our buses rumble off the parade deck.

★

From March Air Force Base we fly to Bangor, Maine. On the Jetway I'm greeted by hunched and knotty but grinning veterans sporting mesh-backed, foam-front caps stamped with geometric military unit insignia. One hands me a Nokia cellular phone. Call your family, he says. Good luck, he says. God bless, he says. Semper fi, he says. I nod and say, Thank you, sir.

I pace the terminal. Families approach other Marines and ask questions. The Marines smile and stoop down to talk to the families' children. The families say they'll pray for us, and even if the Marines are not religious they say, Thank you. No one talks about weapons of mass destruction or oil or justification. I call home, let my family know where I am, ask my fiancée to send or e-mail pictures just so I won't have to talk about war.

I smoke outside the terminal and shiver in the stinging January wind, huddling together with other Marines for warmth.

Charlie drawls, It ain't gay if it's for body heat.

We laugh, press in closer.

I think about what Corporal MacReady said and then think about walking off into the snow. Disappearing into the Great White North.

On the cars idling in front of the airport are yellow ribbon stickers reading SUPPORT OUR TROOPS. I think, I am a troop. Support me. Smuggle me out of this nightmare. I don't want to die for this bullshit. Take me home.

Families reunite, luggage is loaded, gearshifts grind, and I'm left out in the cold.

★

From Bangor, Maine, we fly to Frankfurt, Germany. The airport in Frankfurt provides an entire wing for us. Our new company first sergeant, a lanky black man whose head bobs like a chicken when he walks, stands watch in the gift shop, ensuring we don't purchase alcohol. Some Marines buy cheap airport trinkets. We're all thinking of our families, and trying not to think about what we think we know about war.

I try to sleep across empty airport chairs, but end up wondering instead if I remember enough high school French to get lost in Europe.

The smoking area outside is fenced in with chain-link and topped with concertina wire. Beyond there are people—airport personnel—driving TUGs, hauling luggage, stopping to maybe invite one another to dinner.

Inside I use a phone card to call my family one last time. I have nothing much left to say and so I mostly listen to them breathe one at a time, and even though we've still got thirty minutes before we have to be back on the airplane I say, They're calling us. Got to go.

I cry in a bathroom stall until it's time to board.

*

From Frankfurt, Germany, we fly to Kuwait International Airport. We rally with our squads and then we are sent on a working party to unload the plane's belly of our operational gear in order to reload the gear on a semitruck. We return from the working party. Sergeant Mars calls out the names of our six-man squad to rally us for a sight count of weapons and gear. Corporal MacReady does the same for his squad, as do others.

I am trying not to acknowledge that some of the men whose names were called might die and that it might be my fault.

*

From Kuwait International Airport we board buses to Ali Al Salem Air Base, Kuwait. Our bus passes through a military gate and then minutes later our bus stages behind others in front of a sea of Quonset huts. We file from the bus one row at a time; we rally; we are sent on a working party; we find and stage packs and gear; we reconvene; we count heads, weapons, gear; we count again, and then we are assigned a Quonset hut.

For the next few days I attend formation diurnally to count gear. I clean my weapon, smoke cigarettes, talk about the nude pictures my fiancée promised she'd send as long as I didn't show anyone. I promise to show everyone. I go to the chow hall where they serve sirloin steak and rubbery lobster tail and to-order omelets for breakfast. I jerk off in port-a-shitters and scrawl obscenities with pens or carve them with knives. I count more. I am told to stand by.

I have nothing but time to think about war—about all the people who ever went to war and all the people who never came back. I wish I would've walked away in Maine or jumped the fence in Germany. I feel like an animal in a trap waiting for some hunter to come put a slug between its eyes. I think of wolves gnawing through their flesh and sinew and tendon and bone to stay alive.

Before we left, a Marine I knew shot himself in the foot in a port-a-shitter in Twentynine Palms. He told everyone it was a negligent discharge, that he was holding the rifle muzzle on his boot while taking a shit. We all knew better and we laughed and made fun, but I'm thinking about him now—thinking about the fact that he will get to live and I might have to die. I run my thumb along the butt of my rifle.

★

From Ali Al Salem Air Base we load a C-130 to Al Taqaddum Air Base. The inside of the plane is a gutted whale belly full of cargo nets and canvas seats stretched across aluminum bars and lit red. We are instructed to wear our daypacks on our chests over our flak jackets. The sweatband of my helmet saturates immediately in the C-130. My shoulders touch the Marines to my right and left, my knees touch the Marine's across from me, and if I lean my head back, my helmet collides with the Marine's behind me.

The air is rough; we climb and drop, climb and drop. A few Marines vomit. The stench of fuel and oil and human insides sticks to me, slides down my face with my sweat.

We've been told the muj have the TQ landing strip dialed in, that once we land we should exit tactically—that is, as fast as we fucking can—toward concrete bunkers.

When we land there is no mortar fire, but we still run. There is a part of me that is disappointed, but I am officially in a war and I am smiling by the time we reach the bunker.

★

From TQ we board seven-tons that will take us from Main Supply Route Boston to Route Fran through Al Fallujah to Highway 1 to a small base just outside Camp Fallujah called Camp Mercury.

We leave around 0300 in full gear, our night vision mounted, weapons in condition one. Even with us packed in the seven-tons it is freezing and the convoy crawls for fear of IEDs. The twenty klicks to Fallujah from TQ takes three hours. There are security halts—trash in the road, maybe an animal carcass. Explosive ordnance disposal teams are called. We can do nothing but wait.

Our convoy enters the city and our seniors tell us to stay low, keep our silhouettes out of the slatted windows. The city is dark. There are no streetlights. Cold sewage and bread and tire fires rub against our noses. I can make out the crumbling facades of buildings pockmarked with bullet holes.

One of our seniors says, Shit, wasn't that the building we took down with the MK19?

Heads swivel to get a look; a celebrity sighting. Most of us have seen our salts' home movies from 2004—mortar and machine gun destruction, a corpsman explaining the different bodily fluids seeping from an Iraqi corpse. I am in that world now.

Our berth at Camp Mercury is a massive heavy vinyl tent filled with chintzy metal bunks—our home for the next two weeks until the relief in place is completed. Benito Ramirez, whom everyone calls Cheeks, is one of our seniors. He used to be in our company but was made lead gunner for our battalion commander's convoy and deployed two weeks before us. We see him in the turret of a Humvee as the BC's patrol is about to roll out. He smiles big and strikes a pose, like we should admire muscles he doesn't have, and tosses us cigarettes. We watch the convoy fade outside the wire.

During the days I am busy brushing up on heavy weapons systems knowledge and standard operating procedures and the nine-line medical evacuation procedure and Humvee rollover scenarios.

At night there is nothing but time to think. I think about Indiana and my fiancée. I think about my father, who canceled dinner plans with me before my deployment to attend a work meeting. I think about the letters I used to write my mother in basic training. I think about what life could've been like in Canada or France or how bad shooting myself in the foot might hurt. I think about Corporal MacReady's words. I would rather die than feel the shame of those words. I feel guilty that I don't want to be here, but I feel more guilt about how good it felt running from the C-130 to the bunker. I feel more guilt about how my body buzzed in anticipation when we arrived at Camp Mercury and a Marine told us to be aware of indirect fire and snipers. I feel more guilt when a Marine, enlisted with the battalion we are currently in the process of replacing, is shot through the neck while on patrol and all I can think of is revenge.

I feel guilty because the longer I am here the less I think about my family and fiancée and what life might've been like in those other places, and the more I think about my new family and my loyalty to them and the fear that strikes my heart when Marines are traded between platoons. I do not want that to happen to our platoon, my new family—even though it is inevitable. I feel guilty because I think about laying waste to buildings and entire towns with the MK19 and clearing houses by fire and using my newfound knowledge of the nine-line medical evacuation procedure. I feel guilty because I am not counting down the days until I get home, but the days until we leave the wire and all those gruesome and grisly possibilities move that much closer. I feel guilty because no matter what I feel, I feel like I'm running—leaving something behind.

Turned On by the Fertile Crescent

MASTURBATION IS A MEANS OF survival. Jerking off has saved countless lives throughout countless wars. Probably all the way back to the Norman invasion of England there were peasant soldiers manning the ramparts whacking away trying to stay awake during the night watch. Probably before that. The reason the Trojan Horse worked at all was because some asshole sergeant in Troy's army probably put a eunuch on the wall to keep guard who fell asleep because he couldn't flog the dolphin and, boom, Troy's burned to the fucking ground.

My grandfather wasn't in World War II. So he never talked about it. But I bet if he had been there in the shit, and I could ask him now how he stayed awake in the fighting holes on Peleliu, he wouldn't tell me it was because he was so scared of dying he couldn't sleep or that it was his sense of duty and righteousness.

He'd say, Imagine us, only boys, in fighting holes waiting for the Japs to make a banzai charge in the complete dark on a tiny coral island in the middle of the Pacific. You can't imagine dark like that, Grandson. We hadn't had food or fresh water for days. There was dysentery pooling in our grenade sumps. Got that we were so exhausted we forgot about dying and didn't even know half the time if we were awake or asleep. Some boys, their eyes would close, and they'd wake up stabbed in the gut with a goddamn samurai sword. Fear only gets you so far, Grandson, he'd say.

What really kept all those grunts on point was jerking off to fantasies of Lana Turner and Rita Hayworth and whoever else.

We've been in Zaidon a month and I haven't killed anyone. It's been a month and all I've done is stand on this fucking roof and jerk off. My fastest time so far is forty-three seconds. Mostly I'm too tired to concentrate so I just end up rubbing myself raw for hours at a time.

I'm jerking off when Sergeant Mars walks up next to me and sits in a decaying captain's chair removed from some kind of vehicle.

I don't move; my hand stays on my dick.

What the fuck are you doing, Young?

Sergeant?

I mean, what are you looking at?

I tell him my sector of fire is from the northeast corner of the roof to the southeast corner and that mostly I'm watching the small tree line about two hundred meters out next to the irrigation canal that runs perpendicular to the road leading to the house where we currently reside. My dick is still in my hand.

He grunts. What do you think about war, Young?

It's not like I thought it would be, Sergeant.

Didn't I fucking tell you that? Didn't we all tell all you boots that? Goddammit you don't fucking listen.

I'm silent.

Then he says, You're lucky. We're all lucky. I don't know if you heard about LT and what he did on the last deployment.

No, Sergeant.

He stands up and stretches and out of the corner of my right eye I can see he's not wearing body armor or a helmet.

Fuck, he says. I shouldn't have said anything. I'll go wake up your relief. Who is it? Charlie Beaston? He says Charlie's full name using his impression of Charlie's Oklahoma drawl, like we all do, and in that moment I feel close to him even with my hand still on my dick. And then I wonder if I'm gay and then I know I'm not and then I know if I move my hand now he'll see and I'll never hear the end of the queer jokes and what I think I know about my own sexuality won't mean a thing.

Then there are more footsteps on the roof and a voice.

Sergeant Mars. What the *fuck* are you doing on this roof without your gear?

Sorry, sir. Just checking on Young. I—

I do not give one single fuck, Sergeant. Outside the walls you are not protected. What if we took a mortar round right now? What if there was a sniper? What if we were ambushed? You'd be fucked, Sergeant. Right in the ass.

I don't turn around. I'm still staring out at the field and the tree line and the road and the canal and my hand is still on my dick, but now I'm imagining the LT's geared girth. I imagine he's standing with his hands on his hips and his well-over-six-foot frame is towering over Sergeant Mars's well-under-six-foot frame. I imagine the LT's immaculately shaved face shadowed in the ambient light and his wide monkey mouth and gapped front teeth covered in angry spittle. I imagine all his ass-related innuendos and what he'll change his call sign to next—it's gone from Hammer to Salsa in the time we've been here.

Sergeant Mars sighs.

You better unfuck yourself, Sergeant. Real goddamned quick. These Marines look up to you. Young looks up to you.

There's nothing going on out here, sir, says Sergeant Mars. We're standing here with our dicks in our hands not doing a goddamn thing.

My dick is still in my hand and my platoon leader and my squad leader are squabbling and there are more footsteps and then more voices join and the entire time I've still got my dick in my hand and I'm thinking about those home videos our seniors showed us of Fallujah being destroyed round by round and building by building, of dead bloated bodies, of heat and sweat and blood, and how different my own home movies will be, and how confusing it is to be sad about that, and the arguing is still going on, and my dick is still in my hand.

Coming to Terms

ENTER A MOMENT IN TIME, mid–January 2006, in which a first lieutenant dictates that the end state of his platoon's mission is to disrupt and interdict enemy activity in an area known as Zaidon, specifically in an area known as the Lightning Bolt—three roads whose shape resembles a lightning bolt. Also, in which said lieutenant decides the best way to interdict said enemy activity is to first divide his forces into three sections and then have them cover diverging sectors of the Lightning Bolt on foot, in Humvees, and in a static observation position.

Now enter the moment in which the platoon separates.

In which the dismounted foot patrol steps off at zero four as planned. In which it is February and there are intermittent rains that slow the patrol, put them behind schedule.

In which the mounted Humvee patrol is on the move at its given time to conduct its screen of the area and ultimate extract of the dismounted patrol.

In which, due to slowed progress, the dismounted patrol misses the target extract time and instead is forced to deviate from the original patrol route to meet with the mounted patrol elsewhere.

Now enter the moment in which everything becomes a massive clusterfuck.

In which the lack of situational awareness of the area where said lieutenant's section has only been operating for three weeks becomes as apparent as a festering wound. In which said lieutenant decides to issue a fragmentary order where he dictates that the Humvees are to pull off the alternate supply route and into a fallow mud field and form a coil. Once in this coil, said lieutenant orders the team leaders to drape camouflage netting over their trucks to break up silhouettes.

Now enter an imagined moment in time in which some holes in the FRAGO could have been questioned: How will desert-colored cammie netting break up our silhouettes against black dirt, sir? Should we send a dismounted patrol to clear the area and set an overwatch in those farm buildings across the field, sir? Should we regroup with the observation post before continuing on with the mission, sir? What about the lack of visibility from both the cammie netting and the inclement weather, sir?

Now enter a real moment in time in which the dismounts become surly in the back of the high-backed Humvee—no more than a glorified pickup truck—stuffed together like cold sardines.

In which the dismounts become complacent and leave only one private first class on guard. In which all the dismounts' weapons, aside from the private first class's, are leaning on the outside of the truck so that when whiz-pops start zipping through the cammie netting no one can get to their rifles. In which the back door to the high back is open, and bullets are pinging off it like so much hail. In which there is nothing for the dismounts to do but pile on top of one another and laugh like banshees. In which a lance corporal reaches out to try to close the door and takes a bullet through the sleeve. In which the dismounts all thank whomever they thank that the lance corporal's arms are noodle thin.

Now enter a moment in time in which no one shoots back because no one can tell where the shooting is coming from because of the cammie netting and the inclement weather. In which the spray and pray hits two horses and some goats who scream their dying-animal screams, causing the dismounts to laugh harder to drown out the noises.

Now enter a moment in time afterward in which a plan has gone to shit and confidence in the ability to carry out the mission has wavered. In which the fluidity of the platoon's bodies as well as Command's indifference to the platoon's familial bond becomes apparent. In which, upon examining the hole in the lance corporal's blouse sleeve, all the dismounts begin to understand that it is not just matters of task organization in which they are not in control but all matters concerning their own lives, and that in all actuality they never were in control of their lives—not even as civilians—and that when presented with an infinite number of life scenarios, all those scenarios will end the same.

A New Species of Yucca

THE LEG JUTS UP AT an unnatural angle from a mound of dirt in the middle of the rolling hills of Iraqi-desert hardpan. We have not slept in some hours. We have been rained on for days. We have not been warm in weeks. We are out of the cigarettes Cheeks gave us when we stopped at Entry Control Point Five to stock up on water and MREs. Then we traded our last MREs to a village child, who could have been an adult, for a pack of Gauloises and our makeshift tarp roof collapsed from collected water and soaked the pack. We tried to salvage the cigarettes but the filament-thin paper disintegrated, leaving our fingers sticky with tobacco shavings. MacReady, Fredericks, and Sherburne in the lead truck have cigarettes, but they won't share.

So when we find the leg, we think we might be delusional from any number of things. But the leg is there and we think we can hear one another's thoughts about the leg:

Where'd this fucking leg come from? Why's it in the middle of the desert? Whose leg is it? It's not mine. Is it mine? I bet whoever's it is probably misses it. Is it wearing pants? Think there are cigarettes in the pocket? It is wearing pants. Linen maybe silk—this could be a rich leg.

There is only one leg, so the other unoccupied pant leg is bunched and flopped like a snakeskin on the mound of dirt, covered in mud and camouflaged by the recent rain.

We are in the draw where we found the leg. Behind us is a towering dune of mud and dirt and cracking desert and drying sand. We think we feel the dune shift and breathe and come alive and begin pushing us toward the leg. The leg now maybe resembles something like an altar, where we are maybe supposed to pray. We will fall at the leg altar and prostrate ourselves and throw our hands into the sky and pray to the leg to bring us cigarettes and food and a goddamned resupply.

Then, as we begin to kneel and thrust our arms toward what we think might be our new god, one of us says, Maybe I remember Bible stories about the cradle of civilization between the Tigris and Euphrates. He says, Maybe I'm making up the stories entirely. He says, In the stories Southern California is one of two places where the Joshua tree grows—the other is Iraq. He says, Where the tree grows so exist the earthly gateways to Heaven and Hell, or some shit.

And so we think as the dune at our backs maybe pushes us toward the leg that it might not really be a leg but a Joshua tree.

And then our tired eyes watch the leg begin to sprout limbs and nodules and fronds that resemble smaller legs.

And then we might be falling, but it feels like running. It feels like running because we are covered in sweat. But it is not sweat it is water because it is raining, and we're running and falling while covered in mud toward a voice that might be Jehovah's or Beelzebub's, but might also be Sergeant Mars's, whom we think of as both. The land has faded into the sky and the sky into the land and it feels like we are rising but with every step we still fall just a little, just a smidgeon, just a cunt hair.

Somehow we are back in the truck and our makeshift tarp roof is fixed and we sit across from one another, soaking wet knees kissing, catching on the hems of the reinforced fabric of our camouflaged utilities. Maybe we are thinking or maybe we are speaking or maybe it is just the sound of our teeth and bones chattering but it's all saying the same thing. It comes through in layers compounding one on top of another. Like pound cake and concrete and lung tar and mud and mattresses and tree bark.

Which do you think it was?

Years later, we still ask the same question.

Gambling

Waste Management

IN LATE MARCH WE STAND around our trucks in full gear at Forward Operating Base Black having just received a warning order about a possible one-hundred-man complex attack planned by the enemy to take place at a base in Amiriya. FOB Black stinks like piss-bloated groundwater, mud dust, kerosene, and burning shit. The shit fire at FOB Black smolders around the clock. Command rotates Marines on shit detail. We evacuate our bowels into waste alleviation and gelling bags. They are biodegradable, and the chemical component of the bags solidifies excrement, making it safe for landfills. But because there is no infrastructure in Iraq there are no landfills. Or the entire country is a landfill. We are not sure. The Marines burning the plastic shit bags are from Lima Company. They wear Nomex flight suits and gloves and kerchiefs around their noses and mouths as they walk through the burn pit, a concrete-bordered twenty-by-twenty square that was probably a garden at one point. They dump kerosene in their wakes. While one dumps the kerosene the other four slog on line and rake bags, turning them for even burn potential. They step from the pit and put flame to the bags. The kerosene burns and greasy black shit smoke rises into the air. We wish we could read smoke signals. The doused bags melt and smolder while other bags nearest them swell and bulge with fecal gases. We notice a Marine standing too close and take bets on when and if he will notice the bag in time. The bag bursts, splattering the Marine's legs with hot melted shit. We cheer, shake heads, exchange money, load our trucks, and are on the move.

Thunder in the Distance

We are at the FOB in Amiriya where we have been sent to augment another company of Marines after Command received intelligence about a complex coordinated one-hundred-man attack on their FOB. An attempt to overrun, take prisoners, record beheadings. We ask our seniors what happens if the attack is real. They seem unworried. When we rotate off guard duty we shoot craps for whatever cash we have in our pockets or play blackjack or pai gow. We shoot craps and win and win and win until we don't and lose four hundred dollars. We are not upset about the money, only that we can no longer feel the weight of the dice, their cornered symmetry and indented faces, against our dirty palms. We've been in country since January. It is March and still cold. Somehow even though the air is dead calm, dust plumes tinge our vision to ochre like dried blood. We have a hard time telling when the sun comes up or goes down and we lose track of how much time has passed. Outside we hear what sounds like distant thunder through the stillness and then radio chatter overwhelms our world.

After Action

At Observation Post Mansion we stand in a wide causeway between identical houses on oil-scorched sand sizzling with petrol-smelling cooked meat. Smoking twisted metal stabs the causeway between the geometric gray structures. Outside the building, the Humvees took the brunt of the blast. They are melted metal and fiberglass, bulletproof windshields spider-webbed and dull with fragmentation and soot. Inside the building, glass shards stick into concrete walls, and rebar and chunky mortar litter the floor. A corner of the roof has collapsed, and the sandbags that reinforced the corner are broken open and sagging. No one was killed except the bomber. Ten Marines were injured, four burned—gone by the time we arrived. They were in the Humvees when the suicide bomber blew the cement truck full of hundreds of pounds of homemade explosive dousing their vehicles in flame and shrapnel—the thunder we heard from so far away. Adam, who came to fleet a few weeks after us and was the heart of our mortar team before we were separated into Mobile Assault Platoons, was in one of the Humvees on radio watch. He is all right, but will not—or maybe cannot—speak. The Marines on the roof were taking cover from incoming indirect fire. It doesn't matter. We see ourselves, exploded bits smoking on the sand-turned-glass, impaled and shredded by window shards, crushed by falling rock. What are the odds? one of us asks.

Down the Drain

Back at Camp Mercury we are naked and freezing, vomiting our nerve-racked guts into a porcelain cesspool in a shower trailer that stinks like bodywash and semen and waterlog and dust. We think, Dust is just people with rotten luck. The dead from eons of civilization. Caliphs and Mongolian hordes, Jews and Christians and Muslims, and Husayn ibn Ali, and burned Blackwater contractors and the bullet-riddled Iraqis their ilk shot to death, and there are mothers and fathers and sons and daughters and revolutionaries and radicals and fundamentalists and extremists and suicide bombers. Even them, we think. The shower trailer is their tomb—our tomb. We know we are going to die here, too. Because of anger, retribution, oil, lies. When the power goes out we're left soapy and soaking and shivering in the dark. We can hear the voices of the dead beckoning us: Who wants to take a bet on tomorrow? Who wants to put their money where their mouth is? Step right up. Step right up.

Enemies

THE TWIN BUILDING ACROSS FROM what was once OP Mansion is a husk, an empty flopping lifeless body waiting to be filled and inflated with bones and gases and thoughts and emotions. It is the twin to our beloved, destroyed by a suicide bomber. To make us feel more at home, Iraq has filled the building with sand flies. They are waiting when we arrive and welcome us with grateful proboscises. They wrap themselves around our shoulders and whisper in our ears how good it is that we've come, how excited they are. We are unconcerned with the flies: We have been shot at and blown up; we were just meritoriously promoted; we are big men.

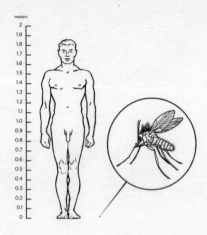

We set our racks along the walls. It is boiling in the husk house. Hotter inside until we go outside and realize we're playing a zero-sum game. Soon, because we are Marines—grunts, crunchies, ground pounders—we fall asleep to the cooing of the flies as they congregate and seem to multiply through our sleep hallucinations.

We itch ourselves awake and shoot our eyes to the walls, indicting the flies, pointing accusing fingers at the small circles of blotchy raised bites, but the flies only do their tiny fly walk and shrug their six shoulders and seem offended we would even suggest they were capable of such a thing.

The game continues for what might be days, maybe years. Inside the husk house days pass like years, but sometimes they pass backward—or up or down. We see Time, a sightless monster made of sand flies with the mouth of a camel spider.

Still, we try to grab it, move Time forward to a moment where this place doesn't exist, to a moment where the entire desert and everything in it has been turned to glass. When we reach out with our raw seeping hands Time explodes into uncountable pieces and covers the walls and we fall back into hazy fevered sleep. When we wake, our bodies are exposed nerves, itching and bloody and distended and we know the flies are more than the hospitable hosts they've made themselves out to be.

The flies are the tide. They are tectonic shift. They are gravity. They break us apart like we are so much kindling, and there is no way to repair the damage they do. The husk house is a terrarium of horror; we are being eaten alive. Our feet and hands split and puss and crust, and sleep does not come. Time is all around us now, its passage unmarkable.

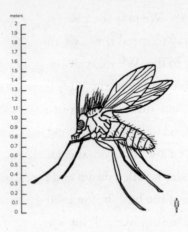

How many hours without sleep, we cannot remember. We burrito ourselves into our poncho liners in spite of the swelter and we sweat and itch and fester. Drink water, says the corpsman. He tells us to change our socks. In the worst cases he gives out Motrin. Somehow it is just us—not the corpsman, not our salts—and we are expected to carry on while our flesh bubbles and rots and bleeds. Our salts make a guard schedule. They overlay patrol routes and continue with life because for them Time has not stopped. For them this is not the husk house of horror, just another patrol base. And so our skin is not the only infected thing—our brotherhood begins to putrefy.

Our salts give us orders and we do not acknowledge. They call our names over and over like overgrown children and we do not answer. We do not ask their permission or their leave, we mutter for them to fuck themselves. We leave our flak jackets open on guard duty, our helmets sit unsecured on our grapes, and our bloated feet no longer fit inside boots so we wear shower shoes. We pray for a barrage of mortars to wipe us away. That's a way to speed time, we think. Death. Everything in life is waiting to die. We are waiting to die. This is our time, this moment, here on top of the husk house with sweat rolling down our faces, our own stink in our noses. We call on high, beg the Mortar God for indirect fire, and there comes the whistle of our death. We close our eyes and spread our arms messiani-cally as the thunder is called down and the earth shakes and the very foundation of the husk house itself might be cracking and splintering—collapsing like a dying star.

When we open our eyes craters smoke in the distance and the house and everyone inside is still living and breathing. That night we cry ourselves to sleep.

One morning the flies are gone. The flies were winning the fight. We wonder where they are, wonder why they gave up. But over the weeks as Time resettles and becomes again linear for our recovering minds and some of our bodies scar forever we understand. The flies weren't winning, they won.

Equal and Opposite

AN EXPLOSIVE DETONATES, BECAUSE THAT is what explosives are made to do. That is the explosive's standard operating procedure. The explosive's SOP. Step one: explosive is built. Step two: explosive is placed. Step three: explosive detonates.

There is little damage to our lead truck, which has triggered the explosive—a blown out tire, some scorching of the steel armor. The explosive was placed too far off the road. We'll learn later that even small blasts needle into our brains, cause slight compoundable concussive incidents. We never blame the blast—that is only what blasts do.

People are inside their homes, have shuttered their businesses. Only an hour ago the shops were open and bustling, people swept dust from dirt, children sold kerosene like we once sold lemonade.

Our trucks halt, because after a blast that is what we've been trained to do. That is *our* SOP. If a vehicle can push through a kill zone, it does. If it is disabled, it stays put and the subsequent trucks disperse to a standoff distance, check fives and twenty-fives, obtain situational awareness and casualty reports, and assess the situation.

A group of men meerkat in the distance and we stare them down with tiger eyes behind thick bulletproof windows. Charlie, next to me, repeats over and over in his Oklahoma drawl, Motherfuckers, which comes out, Muhfuckers. The rest of us say nothing and when the relay comes over the radio that everyone is five by five we rocket open the doors and pursue the meerkat men, because that is what tigers do.

Now there is a man blindfolded and kneeling on uneven rubble-strewn cratered concrete because that is what we do with the guilty after we catch them. We stand around him in an abandoned room that measures fifteen feet by fifteen feet at Forward Operating Base Black, where we've taken him to be interrogated.

We are waiting for the human intelligence exploitation team to arrive so they can question the man. There are two on the team. One is white, the other Arab. This is what I have seen them do to other men: The white man spoke softly in Arabic, he made eye contact, he offered tea and bread. Then the Arab man shouted Arabic. He rolled up newspapers and slapped the men across their faces. Sometimes he used his hands. The white man never stopped his soft speaking.

In the room while we wait for the human intelligence exploitation team, the guilty man attempts to remove the weight from his knees, to settle on his heels. One of us jams a gun muzzle to his spine and moves him back to a high kneel. Behind his blindfold the man whimpers and says, Meestah, please, meestah. We learned the kneeling tactic from John Ta in Third Platoon, who is Vietnamese, and whose father forced him to kneel on grains of rice as punishment when he was young because that is what fathers do.

Into the room walks our Iraqi interpreter, whom we call Rambo because he asks us to and because he carries a large serrated survival knife. Rambo's skin is the color of whipped chocolate. Muscle striations flex beneath the thin flesh of his jaw, which comes to a pointed chin clad in a soul patch. He paces around the man, boxes the man's ears, then kneels next to the man and pulls out his knife.

Rambo is not part of the human intelligence exploitation team, for whom we are still waiting. Waiting is most of what we do.

Our circle shrinks as circles do when something bad is about to happen. Rambo presses the knife blade to the man's cheek and the man speaks quick Arabic. Rambo presses the knife blade into the palm of the man's right hand, which we flex-cuffed behind his back after we tested it for gunpowder residue. He cuts slowly and the man screams because that is what men being cut do.

We don't let Rambo take a finger, though that is what he wants to do.

Hours later the human intelligence exploitation team arrives, they speak with the guilty man for five minutes, and the man is found innocent. We drive him back to his home because that is what we are ordered to do.

Outside the truck we snip the flex-cuffs and remove the man's blindfold and tell him in a language he cannot understand we'll see him next time and then years later when trying to fall asleep we tell ourselves we did what we had to do.

Masks

WE CREATED A PERSON-THING. It looks like us and sounds like us, but it is not us. The person-thing is a by-product—like nuclear waste or babies. The person-thing cannot be uncreated. It is a part of us forever.

Because the person-thing is not human its foremost prerequisite to existence is that we lose not only our own humanity but remove that of our enemy as well. The conditions for loss of humanity were provided amply by the United States Marine Corps.

They said, When I count the cadence you will respond with the repetition *kill* in a loud bloodthirsty manner. 1. *KILL.* 2. *KILL.* 3. *KILL.*

Hajjis, they said. Muj, they said. Targets, they said.

Do it again, they said. You hesitated, now you're dead. Do it again. And again. And again. Now do it right.

For the safety of others, we are warned, the person-thing

into which we may resultantly transform after the creation of the person-thing should be placed in hermetically sealed packaging, by which is meant deep down inside our brain-housing groups. We are given no repetitions or muscle-memory exercises to create a cell for our person-thing. Much later we will be given a multiple-choice health assessment to judge whether we are us or the person-thing. But the person-thing isn't stupid. It can lie. We are told it is good to at least warn our loved ones of the person-thing.

The activation of the person-thing is involuntary. It is an act of self-preservation, an autonomic response to external stimuli. The person-thing is not altruistic; it does not want to save us or shield us—we merely hide inside the fallout from the blast that is the person-thing. The fallout is a shell for our past and future to hide inside.

War is our triggering stimulus.

Provoking the autonomic response of the person-thing in war takes an equal amount of dehumanization and anger directed at us by our targets.

In late March 2006 it takes desperation. It takes fanaticism. It takes belief. It takes a white car—an Opel. It takes untold pounds of homemade explosive. It takes an internal trigger—a pressure plate behind the car's bumper. It takes a collision and a subsequent explosion.

With the application of the external stimulus, the person-thing is loosed. It was frothing in the starting gate and now the shot has been fired.

The person-thing assesses the scene. The engine block of the Opel smolders and smokes on the hood of a Humvee while paint catches fire, flares, and melts plastic and metal alike. In the back of the Humvee the person-thing finds the Opel's transmission. The driver of the Opel is everywhere. Hair and fingers and feet and fat and skin.

Confetti, thinks the person-thing.

The mounds of things that were the driver are more human than the person-thing. A crowd from a local village gathers and the person-thing yells at them. It doesn't matter if the villagers do not understand. The person-thing understands.

On its way to confront the crowd of onlookers the person-thing steps into a fleshy pile and stoops to investigate. It is the suicide bomber's face, blown completely from his skull. It is amusing to the person-thing. The person-thing thinks it is wonderful and hilarious and physically amazing.

It holds the bomber's face in front of its own and screams at the crowd through plump, blood-flecked lips, watching the crowd's reactions through empty eyeholes.

The person-thing thinks of this performance as a warning to the villagers. The person-thing hopes the villagers see its smiling face behind the bomber's rubber one and are frightened.

There is nothing we can do about this. The person-thing returns to its enclosure when it is good and ready. We hide in our shell and wait.

Years later, we discover a picture of the scene hidden away in a box of memories. We feel sick to our stomachs and our legs become restless. We think we need to find a dog to stroke, a baby to coddle. We destroy the picture and reinforce the packaging that houses the person-thing with positive thoughts and exercise and whatever other coping mechanisms we have developed. But even as we rip the picture to shreds and our eyes well with tears for our once-lost humanity, we feel the person-thing slithering along the walls of its makeshift cell, waiting.

Riding the Gravitron

FIRST WE ARE PATROLLING IN our Humvees: Main Supply Route Boston to Alternate Supply Route Iron—I lose track of brown houses and dirty sheep. I am in the lead truck with MacReady, Fredericks, and Sherburne. They needed a dismount. I am sitting behind Fredericks, who is driving. Sherburne is on the gunner platform. From shotgun, MacReady halts the patrol every once in a while to get a better look at some suspicious trash or a dead dog in case of IEDs. We are smoking and talking about maybe quitting.

Then there is noise, but not noise like construction-going-on-outside-of-my-window noise. It is all-around noise. Noise that feels at once everywhere and nowhere. Maybe I'm imagining it. It could be a dream, I think. Like one of the ones that feels like falling and then I wake up at a desk or a table or in my bed, jolting so hard the entire world notices. In what might be my dream my eyes are closed, but not like they're closed in the daytime, when light shines through the thin membrane of my eyelids and gives the dark an orange-rose tint. It's black as pitch behind my eyelids. That's impossible, I think, or maybe it is possible because it is a dream and I really am asleep and that noise is the jolt that's going to wake me up and I'll be back at the patrol base, maybe having fallen out of bed.

That doesn't seem so bad.

We were going to quit smoking.

There's this feeling of weightlessness, too, like being inside the Gravitron I used to ride at the Fireman's Carnival during summers when I was a kid.

And then a blur of things coupled with queasy stomach flip-flops, and I wake up at an aid station, a large one-room tent, partitioned by plywood and paper curtains. I lie on a gurney atop a starchy sheet while Navy doctors cut off my clothes and my boots. I try to tell them, Stop, those are my favorite pair of boots. But they cut them anyway.

It's April and starting to warm up, but we're inside and there's air-conditioning. I'm cold. It feels unnatural, like how people must've felt the first time they saw electric light. My back hurts, my right arm hurts, my head hurts, my right leg hurts.

So, it hadn't been a dream and the noise wasn't part of the jolt that would wake me up and I wasn't weightless because I was riding the Gravitron with my friends, but because—I later learn—our Humvee was flipping upside down. Sixteen thousand pounds of ammunition and engine components and equipment and up-armored steel and people rolling and flipping down a cracked and decaying road in the southern desert outside Al Fallujah.

A male nurse asks me questions, and pushes different places on my belly.

He asks, What's your name? What happened? Where are you? Do you feel nauseated? Did you throw up?

I answer, Matt Young. I don't know. Iraq. Yes. Yes.

I tell him, Turn off the AC. I'm cold.

He jams an IV into my left arm and walks away.

MacReady, my vehicle commander, is the only other person from my truck in the room with me. He's on a cot to my right. A female nurse pushes on his abdomen, and asks the same questions my nurse asked me. MacReady smiles at her, says something I can't hear, the nurse laughs. I watch his hand sneak behind her back and pinch the middle of her left buttock. She swats him away, laughs again, and leaves.

Goddamn, Young, he says. We picked the wrong job.

He tells me after the IED Fredericks and Sherburne got casevaced elsewhere: Fredericks to surgical for brain scans, and Sherburne to Germany. He ain't coming back, MacReady says.

We lie there in silence for a few moments, and I let those words sink in. I just want to smoke, but then thought of hot tar in my throat makes me gag. My head's swimming, the queasy feeling before everything blurred returns, my teeth chatter. I need to call home, I think.

They're going to have to check us for internal bleeding, MacReady says. Hope you washed your ass recently.

What?

It's the easiest way for them to see if you're scrambled up inside. Fractured tailbone's hard to diagnose; it's just quicker than waiting to see if you shit blood, he says. It ain't so bad. Hasn't your girl ever snuck one by you? Hell, I always act like I don't like it, but she knows I do.

MacReady keeps talking about anal stimulation during sex. I hear him, nod and laugh at the right times, but I'm just watching the drip from the IV, feeling the saline flow into my vein.

It's cold like the rest of the room, taking the heat right out of me. The queasy feeling comes in waves.

Before I passed out I was holding Sherburne's head between my knees, trying to stabilize his cervical vertebrae. Our corpsman had taught us that before deployment. Most everyone made some sort of tea bag joke. We'd all laughed.

Sherburne had been thrashing on the road when we'd found him ten meters from the Humvee. The blast had smashed his face into the spades of the fifty cal, and thrown him from the gunner's turret. Half his forehead was hanging down over his right eye, I could see the whiteness of his skull. He kept hitting himself in the face, screaming, trying to put words together that didn't make sense. So I put my knees on either side of his head and MacReady held his arms down and talked to him and tried to make jokes, let him know everything would be all right. I tried to soak some of the blood off his face, take care of the cuts and scrapes, tried to do the first-aid I'd been trained to do. When I touched his face, it felt crunchy, the skin dented in and stayed that way, like a Rice Krispies Treat.

There are footsteps. The male and female nurses are back.

For all his talk, MacReady begins yelling about how they'd better not put anything in his asshole.

They look confused. They tell us we're free to go. They've brought us new cammies and boots. The clothes are clean and don't fit quite right; there are no salt lines or bloodstains, no dust, no mud from fallow fields cakes the knees of the trousers. Like the past months have been erased. I ask for my old clothes. They tell me they've already been incinerated. MacReady asks the woman for two cigarettes. When she turns, he again pinches her butt cheek. She doesn't look back.

Goddamn, he says. We're in the wrong fucking job.

Revision

ON MAY 21, 2006, BENITO "Cheeks" Ramirez is manning the turret when his Humvee rolls over a pressure plate attached to a surface-laid one-five-five round on Main Supply Route Michigan and he dies.

The driver and three passengers are wounded. Our battalion sergeant major, whom we call Iron Mike, loses use of his right eye.

We are not near the blast and so we know none of this in the moment it happens. We only know this after the passage of time, of movement toward the future.

In the future, we want to unknow this information, or we want to travel to the past and warn Cheeks, or tell a story that will somehow bring Cheeks back to life—make him see the bomb in front of his Humvee before the tires compress the pressure plate, complete the circuit—or even raise him from the grave. We want a chance at revision, we want a time-out, a do-over.

In the past, on that day in May, we listen to casevac and quick reaction force calls traveling radio to radio. The calls relay and relay until they become broken and unreadable and we receive mixed accounts of the incident. Our platoon huddles around open Humvee doors, where the radio watch is located at Forward Operating Base Gold. Some accounts report an entire platoon was wiped out. Others report there were no injuries.

The final count is one KIA. Cheeks.

In the future we think, We are the winners of this war, not whoever the fuck we were fighting. We ask one another who we fought. The answers resound: Muslims, Terrorists, al Qaeda, Ragheads, Taliban, Islam, Mujahideen, bin Laden, Hajjis, Farmers, Ourselves. It doesn't matter, we won. If piling their dead like cordwood or sending them to bottomless-pit detention facilities to be forgotten is winning, we won. We came home, they didn't. We have the power. We write the history. We try not to ask what we fought for.

We write, *Benito "Cheeks" Ramirez was manning the turret when his Humvee rolled over a pressure plate attached to a surface-laid one-five-five round and he died.*

We draw a line through ~~he died~~, replace it with *he lived*— strike his death from the ledger, move him into the black.

Nothing happens.

In the past, our salts tip racks and swear and throw their rifles and cry into one another's shoulders. We lament and mourn and say things like, He made it back twice before. And, He gave me a cigarette once. And, Remember when? And, Fucking pointless. And, What for? And, Fuck this. And, Twice before, *twice* before.

In the future, we go in search of Cheeks. Maybe he has appeared in a closet or shed, unaware of the time passed or where he is. He is not there or anywhere. We watch the news, waiting for reports of a long-dead Marine returning home to Texas telling a tale of being rewritten into history.

In the past, the day after his death, at FOB Black, the junked Humvee sits near the burn pit. Light shines through tens of holes in the double-armored vehicle and, though it's been hosed out, there are still stains and coagulation.

In the future, we try to tell the story to our friends and our families. We go to college and try to tell the story. We try to tell the story to our wives. We attend grad school and try to tell the story. The conclusion is always, He made it home twice. No matter how hard we try to rewrite or retell or erase or revise or edit or scrub the bloodstains, Benito "Cheeks" Ramirez's story ends the same.

Hashim Ibrahim Awad

WE MOVE TO HABBANIYA, AN old Iraqi Air Force base. Trashed Iraqi jets spray-painted with American military insignia litter the corners of roads inside the barbed wire compound. The jets are broken and twisted, but the electronics work. The Lance Corporal Underground—the enlisted version of a retirement community gossip ring—tells us that before our arrival, a lieutenant bought himself a one-way ticket when he posed for a picture in an aircraft and pulled the ejection lever, which sent him meters through the air on a doomed flight complete with a complimentary crash landing. He broke bones but lived.

In my rack at night I wonder if the lieutenant thought he might die. I wonder as I fall asleep sweating, mosquitoes in my ears, what dying might feel like.

After some weeks of living at the base we're placed on lockdown. No patrols, combat operations suspended.

Breaking news from the Chatty Cathys in the Lance Corporal Underground: A group of seven Marines and a Navy corpsman murdered an Iraqi man. Hashim Ibrahim Awad. The guy served under Saddam during the Iran–Iraq War, a real old guard motherfucker, the Underground reports. They kidnapped him, took him to a main road, forced him to dig a hole with a stolen shovel, and then wasted him at close range.

Awad was murdered in April. It is May when the Navy corpsman's conscience eats away his fear and he comes forward and the news hits the Underground.

May in Iraq of 2006 is one hundred degrees and never cloudy. May means we've been here five months with another three to go. May is thirty-one days. We have no air-conditioning. We have nothing to do but make ourselves scarce for fear of working parties—painting rocks and raking dirt.

In May of 2006 I watch every piece of pornography ever filmed. After I've watched every piece of pornography ever filmed I run. I run around Habbaniya. It is shaded by date palms and so only ninety degrees. But there is a mile and a half section of flight line that cooks all day, no trees, nothing higher than coyote scat.

I sprint the mile and a half until my breath is ragged, until it feels like my bowels might give way. I pass the junked, decaying jets and wonder what that lieutenant felt traveling toward the vertex of his parabolic flight—panic to elation, and then as the floating in his belly turned to lead dragging him back toward the hardpan, fear.

I wonder whether Hashim Ibrahim Awad ever killed a man in the years between 1980 and 1988. I wonder if he begged for his life, if he cried, if he soiled his *thawb* or whether he said to himself in his head as firing pins collided with bullet primers, *Inshallah*, and closed his eyes.

Maybe all these things.

I pump my legs and think of those men and hate the rat fuck corpsman for snitching and getting us all stuck on this shit hole of a base, and as my vision tunnels to pinpricks the bile and water I retch out of my smiling mouth toward the cracked sand-marbled macadam evaporates in the blow-dryer wind and I think maybe I know what dying feels like.

Self-Diagnosis: How Did That Happen?

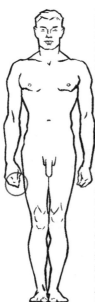

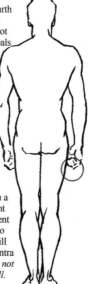

Patient suffers from broken third and fourth metacarpals of right hand. Patient does not recall how metacarpals were broken. Patient insists no alcohol was involved. Patient smells like alcohol. Patient insists it is aftershave. Patient is lying to himself. Patient probably punched a wall or his car or a door. Patient will tell people he got in a fight. Did he get in a fight? Maybe. Patient does not recall. Patient believes it is easier to not recall. Patient will repeat this like a mantra for many years. *I do not recall. I do not recall. I do not recall.*

How to Feel Ashamed for Things You Never Did

WHEN THE BOY RETURNS FROM his first deployment in August 2006, his family is waiting at Camp San Mateo. The company rolls in on charter buses from March Air Force Base in the evening. They exit the buses to a parade deck full of screaming families. Some of his salts who got out before or during the deployment are outside the armory throwing beers over the fence as Marines turn in rifles and heavy weapon systems.

The camp guard gives up.

He finds his family wandering the basketball court at the center of the barracks calling his name. Grandparents, aunt, fiancée—he wants so badly to be happy when he sees them.

The family has rooms at a hotel in San Clemente, California, just outside Pendleton. The boy has leave for ninety-six hours. Four days. The thought of four days with them quickens his heart and sweat slicks his palms. In the car he places his hand to the smooth, cool flesh of his fiancée's thigh, and the muscle beneath her skin tightens for a lightning strike of a second. From the front seat, the grandfather talks about the drive from Mount Shasta to Camp Pendleton. The grandfather talks about driving The Grapevine and the great distances of California and how no one else makes his mochas the way he likes them aside from the chippie at the coffee hut back home. The boy listens, stares at the city lights, and marvels at the lack of tangled wires, at the people walking around after ten at night, at the smiles, at the clean roads.

In the hotel room he drinks beer and liquor and smokes cigarettes. He is quiet at first—the flight from Iraq to Kuwait to California a shock to his system, his synapses are out of whack. He's had a drink or two in the last eight months, only a swig of contraband whiskey here or there. This is something else altogether.

Because of the drink he's tossing down his gullet, later on he won't remember how he began talking about the deployment.

The boy has not lied to them, yet. He tells them stories about Keene hitting himself and trying to talk after their Humvee was blown sky-high by a culvert bomb, about Charlie falling down a dune while taking sniper fire during lieutenant-mandated forced trash pickup, about detaining a twelve-year-old boy during a raid, about being ambushed in the back of a Humvee and laughing.

In the silent spaces between stories, the boy's family filters from the room, excusing themselves to sleep until it's only the boy, the aunt, and the fiancée. The silences hang between them. He sips his bottled beer and moves his eyes all over the room, skipping over the women's faces, which to him look drenched in a sheen of expectation.

What the boy hasn't realized in that moment, what he'll come to understand later, is that the aunt and fiancée are not expecting anything. Instead they're pleading, begging, and screaming for him to shut up, to not crack another beer, to sleep. If he could erase the drunk from his brain he'd notice the facial torsions, widened eyes, crimped mouths. But instead, the warped faces look to him confused and questioning, wondering where the real story is. Like the women are waiting for an answer as to why he has come home this way, nervous and quiet and dispassionate.

So he tells a lie. He tells them about a made-up village and a fantasy house within the village and imagined insurgents within the fantasy house and fictional grenades and bullets used to kill those invented insurgents defending the fantasy house. He tries thinking of realistic films, secondhand stories from his salts, books he's read, anything to tell convincing details of bullet holes and blood spatter and viscera. This feels, to him, like an explanation of individual experience, this black-and-white infallible story of good versus evil. A story where he doesn't feel as though he has to explain his actions. A story where he gets to feel, for once, like a hero.

In the morning, the boy's head aches and alcohol sweat coats his skin like wax. There's a tough, meaty, sick feeling in the ethereal place beyond his stomach, between soul and body, floating around inside—a shattered figurative pelvic bone where he birthed his lie into the world.

The next day in the car on the way to breakfast no one makes eye contact with him. Or maybe it's he that cannot make eye contact with them. Or maybe he's imagining all that. He wonders what he said verbatim. He wonders if he fabricated anything other than his perfect story. Maybe he did. Maybe he didn't. The boy thinks maybe he should ask what he talked about. He wonders if his family would recount the story he told. Will they remember? he thinks. Maybe they'll forget about it, he thinks. They probably don't remember, he thinks. I should tell the truth and apologize, he thinks. I'll just say, Sorry for last night, he thinks. The boy thinks, They'll understand; they are my family; of course they will understand.

He opens his mouth to speak.

The grandfather pulls out of the hotel parking lot in the path of a passenger bus and the boy has a very real, not fictitious anxiety attack. The car shrinks, his ears buzz, his skin prickles. Suspicious roadside trash puckers his asshole, his fingernails sheathe into his palms at the sight of a woman in a hijab. The boy thinks the aunt must notice his reactions because she eyeballs him and tries to make a joke about the grandfather's driving. The boy cannot manage a laugh.

At the restaurant, the family eats, and begins again to talk— family news and gossip, jobs, the fiancée talks about college. Now the boy thinks maybe they never stopped talking in the first place. He stuffs his mouth with huevos rancheros and lets sticky ocean brine into his nostrils for his first full breath in eight months.

The lie becomes a scratch on the roof of the boy's mouth he can't stop tonguing—passively nagging and pulling, closing and reopening, always there. Later, he'll fashion the lie into a story to tell friends, acquaintances, other Marines. After a time, he's ashamed not to tell the story, and that thick sick feeling, in the place beyond his guts in the ether from where the story emerged, becomes a dull throb, a bit of pressure next to his spine or behind his eyes or inside his rib cage, but doesn't disappear, because the boy hasn't found a way for the story to end.

Light Green or Dark Green

WE ARE TOLD THE MARINES don't see race. We hear this in basic training, in movies, during sensitivity training. We are not black or white or brown. We are not even light green or dark green. We are green. We bleed red, white, and blue.

In the fleet we call one another wetback and honky and twinkie and spade and fence jumper and porch monkey and cracker and gook and round eye. We speak in Spanglish and with Charlie Chan Asian accents and Cedric Brown sings slave spirituals as we collect brass shell casings from the desert after firing ranges. Up down turn around pick a bale of cotton, he sings.

And we are told we don't see race.

We laugh and join in with Cedric. Up down turn around pick a bale of hay, we sing. Cedric's body is broad but he has soft almond-shaped eyes and his skin is the color of Concord grapes. He smiles when we sing. He smiles when we run in full gear practicing our movements to contact. He smiles when we are forced to stand in blinding Humvee headlights at night shoulder to shoulder and sing "The Marines' Hymn" before our seniors let us hit the rack.

In the weeks after we return from our first deployment in Iraq, we are drinking at the barracks; happy to be home and happy to be alive and happy that most of our salts treat us now like peers. They give us beers and let us tell our war stories as they once told us theirs.

Do you remember that fucking blast? How about that fucking hajji who shit himself in our truck when we detained him? How about getting bawled out for detaining that kid? Who cares? Fucking muj in training. What about that suicide bomber's face? Like a fucking mask amiright? Remember how Cheeks gave us cigarettes after OP Mansion got fucked? He bummed me a couple at the ECP once.

To Cheeks, we cheer and chug our cans of beer.

Ken Emerson doesn't want to hear our stories. With his rat face he reminds us of Templeton from *Charlotte's Web*. His wavy jet-black hair is receding from his sloped forehead leading into a nose that owns most of his upper lip's real estate. He has silver in his teeth. Back in May, before we first met him, he got cut up by a machete-wielding Canuck at a bar at home in Manitoba— made out with a punctured lung, a damaged kidney, and lacerated liver.

We are on the second deck of the barracks, hanging over the catwalk railing ashing our cigarettes and spewing beers through our noses to the gravel below, telling stories, taking it and dishing it, when Ken stumbles from his room and slurs words in our direction, but we can't hear him for our laughter. Cedric is smiling, telling us about the IED that blew out his eardrum. Lawdy, lawdy, pick a bale of cotton.

Ken puts himself in our faces and says, Fuck you, you think you know about war? Think you been in the shit? He says, You *motherfucks*. You *motherfucks* don't know a thing. He lifts up his shirt and shows us scars. He tells us all, Shut your fucking mouths. Then points a finger at Brown and says, And you, shut your nigger mouth.

Cedric, who always smiles, who invites us to sing slave spirituals with him and smiles, who makes Kunta Kinte jokes and smiles, who took his turn on the Gravitron and got off smiling, knocks the silver from Ken's rat mouth, still smiling. It takes work to tear Cedric away, his knuckles bloodied, his face spattered. There's a stare down between a few salts and us.

You heard what he said, one of us says. You heard him.

They pick up Ken and haul him off.

Another of us says, Mexican standoff.

Another says, Fuck you, *güey, pinche joto gringo*.

We laugh and hit shoulders and get stinking drunk.

The next day as our hangovers peak we remember what happened and spend the next few days anticipating a punishment that never comes.

Years later Cedric will die early of a heart attack in his sleep at home in Georgia. His obituary will tell about the people he leaves behind, his wife and young sons; the awards he won and the character he displayed in combat; after his eardrum was blown out he went back out on patrol the next day. It will not say a word about the night he knocked out Ken Emerson's silver teeth or what shade of green he was.

Lawdy, lawdy, pick a bale of hay.

Meeting the Mortar God

IN OCTOBER 2006 AT MARINE Corps Air Station Yuma, Arizona, on a weapons range with no name in the middle of the desert there is a mountain where the Mortar God lives. He commands, from his vantage, all smoothbore muzzle-loaded high-angle-of-fire weapons and drops imminent death with impunity where he deems it should land. The 81mm mortar crewmen are his favored children. We are they.

As followers of the Mortar God we are fanatical extremists. We live and die by the smell of burnt black powder charges mixed with singed rifle bore cleaning compound. We covet lensatic compasses, scream repetition in tongues as we lay our guns on line in the direction of fire.

The Mortar God's mountain is covered in scrub and loose gravel. Wind scorpions chase our shadows and rattlesnakes shake their bones as we run past. Our bodies sweat beneath our camouflage utilities. Our calves ball and flex and push lactic acid through our quads and hamstrings, our crotches chafe, and our guts clench as the rubber soles of our boots slip on shale and sand and what we assume are the bones of those who came before us. We are elated and panicked and lusty and furious and prideful and strong and monstrous as we run the hill to face the Mortar God.

We have been told once we reach the top to pray and seek forgiveness for the transgressions we have committed to warrant our presence in the Mortar God's domain. We did not check the sights before firing, or we aimed on the wrong stakes, or we didn't punch the bore, or we stacked the ammo incorrectly. We were again meritoriously promoted, this time to corporal, and so we are punished when our squad fucks up. It doesn't matter—we will visit the pain upon them tenfold.

We are to pray with our diaphragms. Push the air from our lungs hard enough for all below to hear, so that they may understand our faults, and in their understanding be purified of their own transgressions. We earned this. We want this. We are terrified. We reach the top, testicles in our throats, flesh crawling with clammy coolness, shaking on unsteady legs.

We invoke the Mortar God. We bellow, beat our chests, strain our vocal cords.

Later, in the desert dusk, we tell stories of his appearance, cloaked in white phosphorus, armored in high explosives, fingers thick as mortar tubes.

It is the Mortar God who bids us, Seek out the second of two strip clubs in Yuma—the one that does not card for identification. Go forth, he tells us. And in my honor defile yourselves. Drink until you've forgotten all fathers before me; drink until you are gone and I am all that remains; drink until you drown.

And we abide because the Mortar God would have it so.

The temple of the Mortar God is named Toppers. Inside it is dark. Hips gyrate and watery, red-rimmed eyes stalk exposed, undulating stretch marks and caesarean scars. Under the strip club black lights our teeth glow like demons and we become a spectacle. Onstage, an exotic dancer fastens a belt around one of our necks for a harness and rides and parades us for the pleasure of the Mortar God. We sweat our drunkenness between the dancer's thighs and breathe in the stink of talcum and body glitter. We dry the taps and empty the bottles and leave in our wake a wasteland of dust and broken glass and bloody knuckles and vomit.

When the lights come on and the place clears out, we're left in the cold desert night beneath the clear Yuma sky and our eyes see twice the number of stars. Double the dead light and double the time. And then we piss in the alley on a trash can while three coyotes watch, heads cocked and ears perked, and we think there might be something to that.

We announce that the Mortar God says, Maybe get a taxi.

In the taxi others ask what we really saw up on that mountain in the middle of the desert looking into Mexico. But we don't answer and feign sleep, because the thing we saw on top of that mountain was far worse than how we'd imagined the Mortar God, and we can't quite find a way to admit that what we saw looked a lot like us.

Future Perfect

IF I DECIDE NOT TO go home and instead turn around and head back to the bar, I will have to retrace my drunken steps the three or so blocks I've already stumbled. But I won't walk, I'll run because I am drunk and because there was a mildly attractive woman—a friend of my platoon mate's wife—hitting on me. She touched my arm and traced my tattoos with a manicured nail, sending shivers into my armpit down my ribs to my ball sack, constricting the flesh and flushing my face. So I'll run. Which means I'll show back up at the bar sweaty from the Southern California aridity, ready for another drink. Those of my companions who never left will cheer momentarily for my return and then resume their conversations or heavy petting or beer chugging.

If I don't order another drink, I will ignore the tacky saliva collected at the corners of my mouth and the tumescence of my tongue and instead walk up the stairs to the outdoor porch seating where the woman is tossing her hair and settling into conversation with my platoon mate's wife. I'll lay my hand on the soft exposed flesh of her upper arm. Startled, she will turn her head, and I'll lean over her face and kiss her. She'll kiss back and I'll grow hard and her saliva will wet my mouth and I'll forget about my thirst and all about my fiancée.

If I go home with the woman, because it's Southern California it will take us an hour to get back to her apartment, which is only twenty-five miles away. It will give me time to sober up. I'll grow tired and groggy and my head will bob and the woman will reach over and unzip my pants and grab hold of me and squeeze and rub and stroke and she'll say things like, Stay with me, and, Make this worth my time, and, Just want to see what I'm working with. She'll follow up with coquettish smirks while keeping her eyes on the road.

If I mention my fiancée, the woman will withdraw her hand and say something like, I'm not into regrets. This will translate to, Shut the fuck up about your fiancée. And so I will, and after a few moments of tense silence and shitty, dated alternative-rock radio I'll move my hand high to the inside of her leg, hitching her skirt in order to feel the humidity between her legs. I'll work my fingers against her panties and feel the stubble at the convergence of thigh and trunk.

If I follow the woman to her bedroom, I will try to psych myself up, to think of witty and sensual things to whisper or growl—the best I'll manage will be, Your hair is pretty. The woman will be all business. When I botch the bra removal she'll say, Stop—it was expensive, I don't want you fucking it up. She'll remove the garment herself; take time to place it in a dresser drawer; leave me sucking in my gut, erection bobbing and wagging, awkward in the dimness. I'll fumble her onto the oversized bed attempting a good mix of assertive and gentle, which will come across as indecisive, noncommittal, and inexperienced. The pressure in my bladder will begin to mount as I slide myself into her, we'll breathe each other's stale breath, and I'll try to angle my head away, suffocating myself in her pillow. My thrusting will be off-kilter and irregular and the woman's hips will buck trying to get control. She'll start to press my left shoulder, a signal I should turn on my back, give her the right of way, and in that moment I'll come without warning and collapse on top of her too ashamed to move.

If I wake up in the middle of the night, in the bathroom after I let loose my uncontrollable postcoital stream, I'll stand in the mirror and antagonize myself like I used to do when I was a child and wanted to cry harder. I'll be disgusted by the woman and myself. I'll think of the stubble between the woman's legs and the razor burn and the imperfections of her body. I'll think about the sex smeared over me and the body smells and breath and sucking sounds conveniently left out of movies.

I'll justify and make excuses and grow angry at my fiancée. I'll tell myself lies: She's probably at school back in Indiana cheating on you, too. It doesn't matter. She has to expect this, she has to know, it was an unspoken agreement. When I end my service in 2009 I'll have a clean slate. I'll be better. I'll quit drinking, smoking, screwing other women. I'll make it up to her, I'll get a job, we'll move to the country—away from people—we'll have each other.

I'll shut off the bathroom light before I open the door so as not to wake the woman. She will be snoring—not lightly. I'll lie on the bed as far away from her as I can and I'll think about my perfect future.

Positive Identification

WE CALL OUR IDENTIFICATION DOG TAGS because of their resemblance to the method of identification used for canines. There is no shyness in the metaphor.

Our dog tags are aluminum, rectangular in shape with convex ends. The five lines of embossed text read:

Last name
First name and middle initial, blood type
Serial number
Branch of service, gas mask size
Religious preference

We wear one tag around our necks on gutted paracord thongs. We wear another on the lower laces of our left boots.

This is the reason we wear the tags: If we are decapitated and our dog tag slides over our neck stumps, our bodies can still be identified. Or, if we're dismembered, if we step on an IED, our legs will be in tatters but our heads and necks will still be attached to our torsos. Ideally.

Our tags are a foretelling of violent anonymous death. They presuppose that death makes us unrecognizable to the living and that while in the Marine Corps the only right way to die is in combat. Most times we choose not to wear the tags—like not wearing them might stop death.

We do not yet realize that nothing stops death—not body armor, or belief, or bravado.

Close to midnight on Tuesday, February 27, 2007, two of us, Baker and Fisher, are returning to Camp Pendleton from San Diego. Fisher isn't the best Marine, he's short with a potbelly, his skin is greasy and pale. Whoever issued his trousers gave him a size too big; they billow around his knees when he runs. Baker looks like maybe he's wearing the utilities that should belong to Fisher. The buttons of Baker's blouse are put to the test. The fabric on the insides of his thighs is pilled and faded. In any temperature sweat runs down his forehead from a fuzzy thatch of mahogany hair.

They are driving from Fisher's girlfriend's apartment, where they had dinner, and where Fisher had a bit too much to drink. Baker is driving, but he doesn't have a license. Baker is sober, but Fisher is asleep. The night is cool, but no matter what Baker does his eyelids cast anchor to his cheeks. The car veers off the interstate in La Jolla, crashes into a tree. Fisher dies instantly. Baker will come to wish he had.

We do not compute. Someone has died, but the person was not shot during combat. The person did not step on an IED. We are not deployed.

In country, 2006, Fisher's vehicle hit IEDs and he lived. He received a Purple Heart, a combat action ribbon. He was no different from the rest of us, but now he is dead. We are still alive. Are we still alive? Are we deployed? Is stateside a dream? Are we still in the shit?

The ground under our feet is spongy, ready to swallow us. We think about dying in war often. We make peace with it. Some of us hope for and invite it. But the rules of death are not supposed to apply stateside. Our numbers aren't supposed to be called unless we are in use like the guns we carry, and like the guns we carry we don't come out until we are necessary, and in the interim it is like we don't exist for the world—for fate, for death. We are well-oiled machines left in the dark, encased in our snug leather holsters, fire selectors on safe. We are not like people and so we do not understand these human moments of frailty.

Confronted by our mortality curling around us like kudzu choking some ancient, mystical tree because we do not know better, because we are like virgins, we let the moment in fully. We experience the loss as if it is the only loss the world has ever experienced.

We become what we are afraid of. We make copies of Fisher's dog tag and wear them.

We hang the tags from the rearview mirrors of our cars. We slide the hanging tags between our thumbs and forefingers, the same way we might one day move our hands through our lovers' hair—gentle and fluttering, a strange touch for men who are trained to take the lives of others.

We wonder if Fisher wore his tag the night he died. We wonder if his girlfriend removed it from his neck and hung it on the opaque conical shade of her small bedside lamp while they fucked behind a closed door as Baker watched television at a higher-than-normal volume in the living room. Maybe Fisher forgot to return the tag to his neck, maybe it's still there hanging on the shade to this day, maybe his girlfriend slides the tag between her forefinger and thumb before she leaves the sleep stink of her mattress every morning.

Or maybe it was never there in the first place.

We have transformed the tags.

Now the tags are acceptance. They are finite life. The tags remind us that we didn't die, but that there are those who did, and regardless of who they were as men they should be remembered. They remind us death shouldn't be feared or welcomed, and that it should be treated with indifference like all inevitable things. The tags remind us it's important to remember instead of trying to forget.

Domino's Tolls the Bell

THERE ARE WHOREHOUSES IN THAILAND. There are women who are paid to massage and bring to climax and send on their happy newly tranquil ways the lonesome, the bored, the curious military boys who wander through the doors in packs like wild dogs begging to be tamed by the perky tits and airbrushed makeup of the civilized world. There are multiple and redundant alcohols one can imbibe if one so chooses, and these libations are served in innumerable bars and exotic dance clubs throughout the land.

And so, gather round and lean in close for there's a story to be told of the days of old, before two wars took up the rotational deployment schedule of the lowly grunt, sentencing countless manboys to time served in the desert. Let's all gather round that man there in the faded green camouflage utilities with the nicotine-stained lips and grim wrinkled face of a gent twice his age. Chances are, he's been divorced, busted in rank, probably has a few kids in different states. The corpsmen at the aid station know him by first name and they keep a stock of penicillin and amoxicillin handy for his frequent visits. We'll listen to his tales in a too-hot barracks room stinking of last night's Yellow Bellies and vomit. It might start out like this: So there I was, hair on fire, balls flapping in the wind, or, You ain't a real man until you get your bore punched. Enraptured, we gather around like children at story time and poke one another in the ribs while the grizzled old bear spits tobacco into a foam cup lined with a paper towel. This magical land he's describing to us full of wanton sex and unmeasured freedom is our future. An all-expenses-paid well-earned anything-goes vacation courtesy of the United States government.

Sure, we might have to spend some days and nights in the jungle, and put up with the golden orb weavers and the snakes, but just think: There's Japan and Thailand and Australia, countries where the mere mention of an American accent sets panties to dripping. No more explosions or deserts. No more jerking off. This is the show, the fuck we've been waiting for.

And then somehow in April 2007 we're being force-fed Domino's on a Southern California parade deck watching our future burst into bullshit. The command throws pizza parties to mask bad news. It's a great opportunity, they tell us. They rattle off the battalion's illustrious combat history. You're warriors, they say between mouthfuls of sauce and cheese. Were we all to contract some mortal disease, they'd stuff our mouths with pizza and smile as we slipped toward the light.

Instead of Oki and Oz and Thailand, our battalion will deploy back to Iraq, back to the desert. Mobile Assault Platoons again. Back to patrolling the exact same fucking roads where we bought our tickets and rode the Gravitron and most of us survived to tell the tale, to the cities where kids tried to throw grenades into our Humvees, to where we piled on top of one another while RPK rounds zipped and pinged around us and we lost our minds with fear so that we could only laugh. We'll go back there and we'll try to do our jobs, but instead, because those things that happened before are no longer happening, because the war—what we think of as the real war—is over, we'll grow complacent and buy sheep from farmers during patrols to fatten and eat, and smoke opium-laced tobacco with out-of-work villagers, and ghost ride our trucks through apartment high rises and post the videos to YouTube and get disbanded and busted in rank.

Then we'll come home nastier and surlier and we'll get drunker than we used to and we'll exercise less and cheat on our wives and fiancées and girlfriends more and we'll have a year left on our contracts. The higher-ups will tell us we'll fail, that we can't hack it as civilians, that we're not civilized anymore, and some of us will give in and re-up. We'll lament their loss, call them lifers, throw them going-away pizza parties, forget they ever existed.

The lifers will deploy with Marine Expeditionary Units and do all those things to the girls in Thailand and Australia we were supposed to do. They'll travel on to their new duty stations and we'll be stuck hanging around, of no use to anybody, short-timers. The command will stick us on the periphery, make us beautify the camp. We'll spend our days Weedwacking and painting curbs red and gold and raking rocks and sweeping asphalt. We'll think of how we used to carry guns and maps and the weight of the world. We'll dream at night of Thai pussy and try to figure a way to get back to the war.

We find it, a call for volunteers. Short-timers wanted to provide security for the colonel of Fifth Marine Regiment in Iraq. Free pizza for anyone interested. So we drop our paint-brushes and Weedwackers and rakes, and we gorge ourselves, stuffing our faces until it's gone. Every last bit.

War Movie

IN THE SUMMER OF 2007 we are broken once more into
Mobile Assault Platoons. Junior Marines are sent to us from
the line companies so we can meet our tables of organization.
Chris, who came to the fleet with us and was a machine gunner
with a line company and then a sniper, joins our platoon.

We train for war at a movie studio in San Diego. Sets built
to resemble villages and homes are constructed to give the feel
of authenticity. Guide wires strung from rooftops to the sandy
ground carry mock-RPG explosives as they rocket toward our
patrols. A loudspeaker atop a minaret at the fake village center
plays the *adhan—Allahu Akbar, Allahu Akbar*—over and over,
never the *shahada*. It is maddening. Women shuffle around in
burkas; most have some kind of weapon under their shapeless
garb. We are told to treat everyone with courtesy and respect
but always have a plan to kill them. We are told the rules of
engagement and reminded about escalation of force. We are

told we are professionals and should conduct ourselves as such. We are told we are here to win hearts and minds. We are told we cannot search women, we are told we cannot make physical contact with the actors, and we are told the actors will follow the rules. It's all just a cunt hair away from being real.

The studio has hired former Navy SEALs to help train us—to be our aggressors. They hire actors and stagehands and special effects gurus and advisors and coordinators and amputees. In a large room we sit with our left hands on our left knees and our right hands on our right knees. We act professional and serious—how we've been told men going to war should act. We fall into single-file lines and give mission briefs like robots. We rotate in and out of activities with other platoons, a round-robin of military operations.

There is a village, a school with movable walls, and there is a kill house—set up for cordon searches, cordon knocks, and raids. Inside, actors and former special forces operators crouch in wait with their weapons augmented to shoot 9mm paint rounds that sting like wasps. There is a woman who we call Lara Croft. She carries Desert Eagles akimbo and dives for cover across hallways, shooting at us with deadeye accuracy from behind her burka. We all die.

When RPGs in the village impact near an amputee someone behind the scenes presses a button and the woman's leg explodes into spaghetti-like gore. When a sniper uses a second-floor window in a building facade to plink blank rounds in our direction a controller walks around in the room we are huddled in and douses some of us with fake blood and says, You're dead. You've been hit in the femoral. You have a sucking chest wound. Our corpsman goes to work and the call to prayer blasts our eardrums to dust.

In the school with the movable walls we come to a T intersection in a hallway. One of us is shot, another is taken hostage. We spend the next fifteen minutes pinned down while an actor sprays us with paint rounds. Our command watches from catwalk vantage points, they make calls over the radio, deny casevac and QRF, they make it impossible for us to survive to see what we will do.

One of us has an idea to throw a blank grenade—a glorified blasting cap—calling, Flash bang out! We rush in to save our comrade and detain the actor.

During the debrief we are chastised. You can't get pinned down like that in a house, they say. You should've thrown a grenade around the corner, they say. Your buddy would've been dead already anyhow, they say. Got to think quicker, they say. Sometimes you've got to make sacrifices. Train for the worst, they say.

We have been mortarmen too long. We have forgotten what it is like to be door-kickers. Chris, who was birthed a grunt, helps remind us.

Fuck this, he says.

Soon we are running behind sets and climbing catwalks and putting our knees into the actors' throats and placing them in incapacitating holds, wrenching their arms and bending their knees and tackling them to the ground. We are hissing Hajji and Muj in their ears and putting the soles of our boots into their faces.

We are showing them what real is.

One junior Marine, whose Kevlar helmet is too big and whose belt is missing a loop, we call Lawrence. Lawrence is gentle. He leads detainees by their elbows.

Lawrence, you fucking boot, we say. You are in a world of shit. Watch us.

We shove our arms up under flex-cuffed wrists and grab the napes of necks, putting shoulders to the test. The actors grunt and cry out and some fight back and get into it and some say stop. It doesn't make a difference.

Between stations we jerk off in overflowing port-a-shitters and draw giant veined cocks on the walls, proclaiming in graffiti, *The Green Weenie Was Here* and *Chesty is Watching* and *BOHICA*.

We want to burn the world down. We want to kill and die and make up for not killing or dying in 2006.

We are sick of acting.

Down the Rabbit Hole

YOU SPEND A MONTH IN June 2007 at Marine Corps Air Ground Combat Center Twentynine Palms outside Palm Springs, California, during Mojave Viper Combined Arms Exercise in one-hundred-plus-degree heat. You try to escape the heat to a port-a-shitter where you go to town on yourself, using your sweat as lubrication. It stinks of shit and desert and diesel and your pupils pin in the rose light sneaking through the blue plastic coffin air vents, turning the horror into a 1980s porno boudoir.

You are thinking of war death destruction bleeding bodies heroism medals fantasy blow jobs anal sex intimacy. Your brain flips pages, parts the reeds searching for what it needs. You are thinking of exes, one-night-stands, the female engagement team that's currently training with your battalion—the existence of which Command has told you not to acknowledge. Abdominals strain, your body pushes forward through memory.

A fly lands on your upper lip and you blow it away but now you're thinking of shit. Shit everywhere, the fly covered in the insides of your platoon mates now all over your face, burning shit, black oily smoke in your nostrils and still somehow you're hard and plugging away, drilling through gray matter to the archived log of sex acts notable enough to get you off all these years later.

Outside, voices drawl about pussy and beer and cigarettes and dip. There's a group of who-knows-how-many singing an '80s hair band ballad while you treat yourself like a lawnmower's pull start. You wonder if there is something wrong with you— if there's something in you that's broken, a chewed gear or rusty bearing. That would make your actions easy to explain, some dark part of your past you've sequestered into the ADULTS ONLY section of your brain. It's not that easy.

Focus, think of your fiancée, the pictures she sent, the sex you've had, the places you've had it, and you're almost there, but she's not with you, she's hundreds and thousands of miles away, and her face twists, morphs into the girl who blew you in the alley behind the bar two weeks ago, now she's a young female Marine from a month before who you fucked on your friend's bed, now she's the friend of your platoon mate's wife, now she's two college girls at a house party in San Diego, now she's your ex-girlfriend, now she's your ex-girlfriend's friend, now you're breaking into your fiancée's ex's house after he sent her an innocuous text message and beating him as he sleeps, now you're going down on a girl who is not your fiancée in a bathroom, now you're lying to your fiancée and telling her she can't go to a party because it's at a bar and she's not twenty-one and it's really not at a bar but your platoon mate's wife's friend is there and you're thinking maybe you can talk her into a for-old-time's-sake blow job. The lies are compoundable; they meld with the shit air of the hotbox, morphing into a physical presence. Bulbous and veiny through it all you're cranking away, debriding a wound, cleaning the grit from avulsed flesh after the car wreck into which you've turned your life.

Humvee engines turn over, growling for your blood and you pump your arm through a spasming bicep chafing and grating. You hear your name riding Humvee exhaust to your ears. The sweat stings now and you know you've got to finish, that if you don't you are wrong and you are bad and your scale is off balance and you are in the red—but if you finish you can still turn this all around, you can still make your relationship right, you can spend your married years making it all up, throw yourself at her feet, lick her boots clean, offer her your manhood.

Maybe that will be enough.

You explode into the blue hell below your knees, not your spunk, but you, shot from the tip of your own miserable prick, accelerating from zero to forty-five kilometers per hour, soaring past your lies and all those other women and affairs toward whatever kind of misery waits for you.

How to Ruin a Life

Step 1: Start out with something to prove. Join the United States Marine Corps, become senior enlisted Marine.

- These may seem like separate steps, though be assured they are one and the same; it's merely what you're setting out to accomplish that differs. For instance, you might have something to prove and in rebuttal to that feeling of inadequacy you might paint a masterpiece or get a PhD. However, you'd be doing the wrong thing if you wanted to ruin a life. You might be following the steps for "How to Get Revenge by Living Well" or "How to Become a Better Artist."

Step 2: After a deployment to Iraq, develop a serious chip on your shoulder and an inability to compromise.

- You'll be ambushed, you'll be blown up, you'll be afraid and tired and cold and hot and lonely and miserable.

- You'll never see the war your salts tell you about.
- You'll never get to kill another human.
  - You'll feel cheated by this.

Step 3: Use rank and privilege to hold junior enlisted Marines to an unfair standard.

Step 4: Drink. A lot.

Step 5: Be as unsympathetic as possible—remember that chip.

Step 6: Target the most emotionally vulnerable and impressionable person you can find. Become his mentor. Become the person he should trust and turn to, the person who should have his back.

- This person will have:
  - Anxieties about transitioning into military life.
  - A tumultuous home life.
  - An unhappy spouse.
  - An eight-month-old baby.
  - Trouble getting to work on time.
  - Difficulty remembering Marine Corps customs and courtesies.

Step 7: Exploit everything wrong with this person instead of tapping into your ability for empathy.

- Feel free to point these faults out to others and encourage them to point out faults they find with this person as well.
- Refer to this person as Lawrence in reference to the massive fuckup from *Full Metal Jacket*, Private Leonard Lawrence.

Step 8: Drink some more.[1]

Step 9: Find a "last straw" with your charge.
- Should be something arbitrary:
  - A missed belt loop.
  - Sloppily rolled sleeves.
  - No fresh haircut.

Step 10: Blow this discrepancy out of proportion.
- Relate this thing to combat and his inability to complete simple tasks.
  - E.g. an improperly looped belt shows a lack of attention to detail, which will result in this person causing the deaths of Marines in combat.

Step 11: Proceed to physically intimidate.
- Interpretations will vary but may include:
  - Threatening language.

---

1. Read: excessively.

- ○ Physical contact with this person's body.
- ○ Physical contact between this person's body and an inanimate object.
- Encourage others of your same rank and privilege to join in.

Step 12: Act unsurprised when this person does not show up for work the next day.[2]

Step 13: Act even less surprised when Mexican authorities discover this person transporting illegal immigrants into Southern California.

Step 14: Be completely unaffected upon hearing that during his transportation back to Camp Pendleton on September 22, 2007, this person managed to slip the zip ties binding his wrists and open the sliding door of the van traveling at eighty miles per hour down the Five.

- Remain similarly unmoved on learning he jumped.

Step 15: Now live with it. Go on. Try to live with it.

---

2. Or for the rest of the month.

All of the Above

AT THREE IN THE MORNING during the summer of 2007 you are on a drunk so heavy you'll manage to erase the previous week of temporary assigned duty at Marine Corps Air Ground Combat Center Twentynine Palms. You'll patchwork it all together later. You're attending a course in electronic countermeasures—devices that interrupt signals from radio-controlled IEDs. It is the night before your final electronic countermeasures test and you and six of the ten Marines in the course are strewn about an apartment after a night of barhopping in Palm Springs, California.

The apartment belongs to a woman who was a bartender at a club you hopped named Zelda's. She has invited some of her friends over. While you are running your hands over the body of a fit Hawaiian woman who is not your fiancée but is friends with the apartment's renter, it hits you that:

A. You are about to deploy again to Iraq in less than two months.

B. You are an incompetent leader and a substandard Marine.

C. You are a cheater and liar and borderline alcoholic.

D. All of the above.

The Hawaiian sits on your lap and leans back against your chest. You are thinking of:

A. The way the thin cotton blend of her dress clings to her curves.

B. The feeling of the split of her ass against your crotch.

C. Your fiancée, who will come to visit you in a month to see you off to war again.

D. All of the above.

Over the Hawaiian's shoulder you decide:

A. That the apartment lacks furniture but is clean.

B. That what the apartment lacks in seating it makes up for with walls bright with photos and art.

C. That imagining yourself in the photos of the women's friends who are smiling and laughing on the beach, at bachelorette parties, and during movie nights makes you feel like you are home. Resolve never to leave.

D. All of the above.

In the living room there are three women and five men (including you) scattered across a couch and the floor. The men are your fellow NCOs. Three of them are drunk. One of them is a designated driver who has taken his job seriously. Where is the sixth?

A. Passing out in the twelve-passenger van you personally drove from Camp San Mateo to Twentynine Palms.

B. Vomiting in the twelve-passenger van you personally drove from Camp San Mateo to Twentynine Palms.

C. Pissing his pants in the twelve-passenger van you personally drove from Camp San Mateo to Twentynine Palms.

D. All of the above.

One of the women in the living room asks what you think of the war in Iraq. You act like you don't hear the question and after some silence the conversation in the living room turns toward the "never have I ever" and "prove it" variety. Your mind wanders to the road trip from the fresh summer sting of the coast to the shit hole of Riverside then through Joshua Tree National Park just before hitting the interior Marine Air Ground Combat Center Twentynine Palms. You begin to think about:

A. How you should think Joshua Tree is beautiful—most people find it beautiful. But all you can think of is your first deployment to Iraq when you were so tired you might've hallucinated a leg that might've been a Joshua tree that might've not been there at all in the first place but was probably a leg.

B. How Joshua trees apocryphally represent the gateways between Heaven and Hell, and if Iraq is Hell by proxy—because of course Iraq would be Hell—does that make

Twentynine Palms Heaven? Or maybe that's all wrong and California is the host of an interdimensional Hell portal. Maybe they both lead to Hell. Maybe that's the joke of it all.

C. How you are about to deploy. Again. To Iraq. Again. How since your promotion to corporal and most of your seniors reaching their end of active service you and the boys you came to the fleet with—John, Chris, Charlie, Adam, others—have been expected to lead. How you're one of the men your Marines look to. You repeat the phrase in your head: *your Marines*. You think about how you are a better follower. How you've always been a follower. How you should've remained a follower. How if something goes wrong now it's all on you. How there is never any escaping that feeling.

D. All of the above.

The bartender from Zelda's takes a Marine into her bedroom. The designated driver looks at his watch and furrows his brow, though he tries to laugh at the story that's been told three times already: When hopping bars one of the sergeants you were with reached over the chained-off section of an open-air restaurant and interrupted a date by taking a handful of fries being shared by the couple, and then proceeded to enter into their conversation seamlessly. The couple thanked him for his service. The bartender and the Marine reemerge. Everyone makes jokes about hitting and quitting and two-pump dumping. The designated driver uses this as an excuse to corral you and your drunken comrades. The Hawaiian pushes her ass into your erection and asks you not to go. She says, Let's just go to sleep. I'll make you pancakes in the morning. What do you do?

A. Make a stand. Incite a riot. Curse and swear at the designated driver. Decide to go absent without leave if only for pancakes. Say, Fuck the Marine Corps. Say, I don't want to go back to Iraq. (It will be the designated driver's first deployment to Iraq. Before this he was a security guard at Guantanamo.) Call the designated driver a boot. Call him an inexperienced child. Tell him to go fuck himself. Tell him you're staying. Tell him he can go on and die if he wants to.

B. Give in. Stand to say goodbye to the Hawaiian. Hug her and caress her perfect ass. Turn her around so that her back is to you; let her grind into your crotch again. Let her loll her head back under your chin and then stoop down to slobber her neck, take in her scent like the dog you are. Move your hands to her breasts. Don't think about the other Marines or the women or your fiancée or your family. Think that you might die again. Think no one is lucky enough to escape a second time. Think of Cheeks. Think you want to feel life and fucking is a way to do that. Pull the hem of the woman's skirt up to see she's not wearing underwear and then hear her scream and feel her palm connect awkwardly high on your cheekbone and smash the tip of your nose.

C.   Remember you are a follower. A coward. Sulk to the van. Curse the designated driver. Pass out as soon as you hit the seat. Wake, still in the van, still drunk, to the smell of stale tobacco and vomit and cheap tequila with no memory of what happened. Take the trip to the classroom where your test will be. Take the electronic countermeasures Scantron test and pass. Take the electronic countermeasures practical application test and pass. Receive a certificate of completion. Think about what it means to pass a test drunk. Wonder if this is what college would've been like. Drink a gallon of water. Load the van. Travel the three hours back to Camp Pendleton. Stay awake until Joshua Tree National Park. Think about your first deployment. Imagine a forest full of exploded, charred limbs cracking and splitting in the sun. Feel nauseated. Think about Sherburne's crunchy face and the way a man cries for his family when he is being tortured. Fall asleep and dream about the desert.

D.   All of the above.

Packing Level: Expert

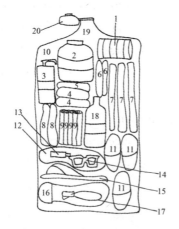

Equipment and Gear You'll Actually Bring and Use:

1. Half Log Copenhagen Long Cut
   - For:
     - i. Barter
     - ii. Late-night post
       1. Cigarette cherries are good sniper aim points

2. Protein Powder
   - For:
     i. False sense of accomplishment
     ii. Meal supplements
3. Lotion
   - For:
     i. Masturbation
     ii. Dry desert skin
4. Sweatshirt/sweatpants
   - For:
     i. Warmth in winter months
        1. No one ever talks about how cold the desert gets
5. PT Shorts
   - For:
     i. Running
     ii. Quick-drying underwear
6. Civilian Clothes (T-shirt, basketball shorts)
   - For:
     i. Sleeping
     ii. Attempting normalcy
7. Three Cartons of Marlboro Reds
   - For:
     i. Smoking
     ii. Barter
8. Utilities, Desert
   - For:

      i.   Clean clothes

     ii.   Because you're not a complete shitbag and want to set a good example for junior Marines

9. Porno Mags
   - For:
     i.   Masturbation
     ii.   Leisure reading
     iii.   Morale boosting
     iv.   Wall decor

10. Self-loathing
    - For:
      i.   A reminder of your first deployment to Iraq
      ii.   Impeding work performance
      iii.   Increasing cynicism
      iv.   An excuse to drink
          1.   Alcohol ultimately makes things worse

11. Skivvy Eggs (socks, shirts, skivvies made into a ball)
    - For:
      i.   Easy transport
      ii.   Self-containment
      iii.   Construction fun!
          1.   To make: Fold skivvies (undershirt, underpants) into small square, place feet of socks in center, roll up so cuff and leg are exposed, fold cuff and leg over rolled up shirt and underpants

12. Running Shoes

- For:
    i. Running
    ii. Other exercise
    iii. Attempting to keep feet healthy
13. Thumb Drive, Loaded with Digital Porn (inside running shoes)
    - For:
        i. Masturbation
        ii. Boredom
        iii. Because you've got a problem
            1. Add it to the list
14. Extra BCGs (inside running shoes)
    - For:
        i. Accidentally fell into your shoe, did not intend to pack
15. Shower Shoes
    - For:
        i. Comfort
        ii. Avoiding stepping in semen in shower stalls
            1. Because Marines jerk off in the shower (when there are showers) and no one wants to step in someone else's spooge
16. Extra Boots
    - For:
        i. Avoiding ass chewing about how nasty your combat boots are on the flight back

1. This speaks to the fact that you believe you will indeed make it home
2. Your optimism isn't dead yet
3. Congratulations

17. Dog Tags
    - For:
        i. Easy identification of body if maimed, killed, or incapacitated
            1. Place on chain around neck
                a. In case of dismemberment
            2. Thread low on left bootlace
                a. In case of decapitation

18. Vodka (in misleading water bottle)
    - For:
        i. Borderline alcoholism

19. Shoulder Chip
    - For:
        i. Feelings of inadequacy as a Marine and a man
            1. You've never been in a firefight, never killed another human
            2. Your seniors fought house to house in a city—what did you do?

20. Combination Lock
    - For:
        i. Avoiding the sticky fingers of other Marines
            1. Gear adrift is a gift

Rabid

IT'S IMPORTANT TO REMEMBER THAT "dog" is a loose term. It's important to remember that we can say they probably most likely without much of a doubt and with the utmost confidence all have rabies or worms or congenital diseases or are overpopulated or are suffering from canine depression or have bitten a village child or whatever. It's important to remember our boredom and lack of sleep and anger and sadness and youth and misunderstanding and loneliness and hate. It's important to remember that we don't want to, not really, not deep down. It's important to convince ourselves of this especially. It's important to remember that we're just following orders. It's important to remember the Nazis and the Nuremburg Defense.

It's important to remember that we're stuck in the gray cracks between black and white where answers are like handholds in a wall of obsidian in the dead of night. So before we aim in we think again about rabies and overpopulation and safety issues for the denizens of whatever the fuck Iraqi village we're driving past, but we can feel our pulses quicken and our skin tighten and we even feel our pupils slam to their outermost border, dilating, taking in the night.

It's important to remember that we have a dog back home that sleeps in our bed and pees the floor it gets so excited to see us. It's important to tell ourselves this. It's important to say, We don't hate dogs, and then remind ourselves that these aren't really dogs. They're not our dog.

It's important to know the statistics of people who commit cruel acts in regard to animals and how those acts may correlate to sociopathy or to domestic abuse or to myriad other psychological disorders, which come with a loss or lack of empathy. It's important to plan for the future. It's important to not take pleasure in this.

It will be important to justify the choices we're about to make. It will be important, when telling this story, of how we shot dogs in Iraq, while drunk in a bar years from now that we sufficiently lower our head and hunch our shoulders and talk in a low voice about how we never wanted to, that we didn't have a choice.

It's important to follow weapons-safety rules. It's important to remember to never point our gun at anything we do not intend to shoot. It's important to keep our weapon on safe until we're ready to fire. It's important to keep our finger straight and off the trigger until we intend to fire. It's important to know our target and what lies beyond.

It's important to understand bullets don't stop just because they hit something.

It's important to remember, now that we've moved our selector lever to fire and our finger begins the slow steady squeeze we've practiced to the point of permanent muscle memory, that when the bullet stops, it won't really stop. The bullet will travel through the dog and maybe through whatever is beyond it, or maybe become lodged in large bone or lost in the thoracic cavity.

Whatever the bullet does, it will be important to know that once it leaves the chamber, its true path of trajectory will pass directly into us, where it will ricochet off our bones and rip through our insides and smash into our consciousness. We will not feel it in the moment, but it will be bouncing and tumbling and shredding for years.

It's important to help the bullet exit so the wound doesn't fester and swell and leak puss and poison our blood.

It will become important to support no-kill animal shelters in hopes of aiding the exit. It will be important to donate two dollars for every trip to the pet store. It will be important to purchase for our own dog a designer dog bed filled with memory foam, and all-natural dog food, and preventative joint damage medication, and enzyme toothpaste to ensure healthy gums and teeth, which ultimately helps to avoid heart disease. It will be important to upset our own life and not board our dog and write pages upon pages of instructions for those watching her when we absolutely cannot do so.

It's important to remember that the exit will leave a secondary wound as exiting bullets do. It will be important one morning after waking from a nightmare in which we are being torn apart by snarling, rotting dogs to look into our dog's sweet sad sleepy doe eyes and attempt an apology that's meant not just for the dogs but for everything we did are doing and might someday do.

How to Build a Raft

Orientation: Camp Baharia, old Baathist resort town favored by ones Uday and Qusay Hussein, southeast of Fallujah, November 2007. Sixty days into deployment two.

CAMP BAHARIA OVERVIEW

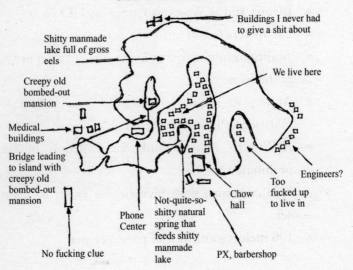

Buildings I never had to give a shit about

Shitty manmade lake full of gross eels

We live here

Creepy old bombed-out mansion

Medical buildings

Bridge leading to island with creepy old bombed-out mansion

Engineers?

No fucking clue

Phone Center

Not-quite-so-shitty natural spring that feeds shitty manmade lake

Chow hall

Too fucked up to live in

PX, barbershop

- Lake may contain unexploded ordnance from U.S. bombing of area
- Local mythology: Uday, who had penchant for kidnapping young girls, preferred transport of victims to resort home on island in middle of lake
  - Girls raped, murdered, weighted, thrown off dock
- Local mythology: lake populated with freshwater eels that feed on corpses of said raped, murdered, weighted girls
  - Explains size of eels

Situation: Enemies, friendlies, attachments, detachments, neutrals

- Enemy forces/hazards:
  - Weapons Company Higher Command
    - Bivouacked at Weapons Company HQ
    - 250 meters east of current position
    - Ability to impose office hours for violation of lake prohibition
    - Ability to impose nonjudicial punishment for violation of lake prohibition
    - Ability to remove rank for violation of lake prohibition
  - Asshole corpsmen with bivouac site closer to phone center
    - 100 meters southwest of phone center

- Ability to make higher command aware of illegal activity (e.g. entering lake)
- Ability to remove comfort items: Motrin, Ativan, etc.

o Army assholes have bivouac site closer
  - 350 to 400 meters northeast of phone center
  - Potential for friendly fire as per Army Guard incident in 2006
  - Quick to trigger
  - Best to avoid

o Unexploded lake bombs
  - Still have explosive potential???

o Lake
  - Could fall in
    • Not sure how deep lake is
    • Full of eels
      o Saw one breach other night. Thick as forearm. Might have been longer than I am tall

• Friendly forces:

o Operators: Chris Smith, hereby referred to as Echo-3 Sierra, and Matt Young, hereby referred to as Echo-4 Yankee, Mobile Assault Platoon 3A

o Remainder of Mobile Assault Platoon 3A
  - Currently at bivouac site 4 klicks from objective and enemy
  - Remain behind element unaware of operation

- Attachments:
  - None
- Detachments:
  - None
- Neutral forces:
  - All others in vicinity of bivouac site
    - MAP 1A
      - No qualms
    - MAP 1B
      - No qualms even though has most guys from Texas
    - MAP 2A
      - Least trusted
      - Reckless
    - MAP 2B
      - Even less trusted
      - Idiots
    - MAP 3B
      - On good terms
        - Regardless of what Echo-4 Whiskey said other day . . . can go fuck self
        - Regardless of Echo-4 Delta's posh British fucking accent and that he's probably gay
          - Everyone's gay in the field, anyway

Mission: To build raft out of found material and cross channel between our bivouac shore and phone center shore for easier more accessible route to phone center to call family, women, friends.

THE SHIT THAT MATTERS

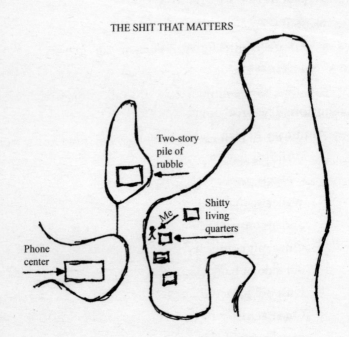

- Reason:
  - 4 klicks too far to walk in cold rain
  - 4 klicks too far to walk when dark
    - Time difference dictates must go at night
    - Operations dictate must go at night
  - Bored
    - So bored

- Threw rocks at hole in concrete today for three hours, made one rock, feel good about progress, should be improvement tomorrow
  - ○ Side mission to find place to drink bottle of vodka sent from stateside
    - Would like to get drunk
      - Safe???

Execution: The breakdown
- Summary of plan and concept
  - ○ Will first have to gather supplies to make raft
    - Parts, tools, etc.
  - ○ Will also have to find place to hide raft while not under construction
  - ○ Once raft completed will tie paracord to date palm on our side of bank and then paddle to far bank
  - ○ Unspool paracord during crossing
  - ○ Once across will tie paracord to large boulder from wreckage of Uday mansion
- Breakdown of duties
  - ○ Echo-3 Sierra
    - Design raft
    - Gather parts for raft
    - Construct raft

RAFT MATERIALS

SIX (6) HUMVEE TIRE
INNER TUBES

4'×6' PLYWOOD
PLATFORM

TWO (2) 2"×4"×36"
BOARDS   4"
           2"
36"

6'
4'

ONE (1) SPOOL 550
CORD

VIEWS OF RAFT

RAFT: BOTTOM VIEW

RAFT: TOP VIEW

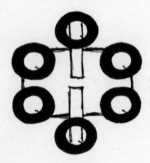

- Echo-4 Yankee
  - Gather tools
    - Hammer
    - Nails
  - Supervise
  - Some construction

- • Make paddles
- ▪ Will mostly supervise
- ▪ And bring vodka

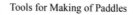

Tools for Making of Paddles

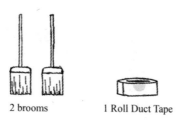

2 brooms   1 Roll Duct Tape

Construction of Paddles

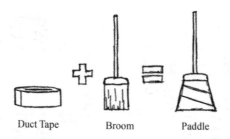

Duct Tape   Broom   Paddle

Admin and Logistics: Supply, evac, transport, misc.

- • Supply
  - ○ Food
    - ▪ Chow hall
      - • 350 meters southeast of position
    - ▪ MREs
      - • Next to NCO hooch

- ○ Tools
    - ▪ Located in toolboxes in most trucks at our disposal
- ○ Weapons
    - ▪ Not required for mission
- Evacuation Plan
    - ○ Should bodily injury occur BAS located 3.75 klicks from current position
- Transport
    - ○ No insertions/extractions
    - ○ Foot mobile
    - ○ Raft
- Misc.
    - ○ None

Command and Signal: Signal instructions, commander position

- Signal
    - ○ None
- Commander position
    - ○ As Marine with longer time in grade, Echo-4 Yankee will take form of commander
        - ▪ Let it be known, most work credits and creative license revert to Echo-3 Sierra

After Action: Debrief

- Problem: People don't always answer the phone

- Solution: Get drunk
- Problem: Being drunk caused one of us, maybe Echo-3 Sierra (who Echo-4 Yankee thought had the line and whom Echo-4 Yankee asked, Hey do you have line, and thought Echo-3 Sierra answered, Yeah, I have the line) or maybe Echo-4 Yankee, to drop the line in water
- Solution: Use paddles to get back to shore
- Problem: One of us, maybe Echo-4 Yankee, maybe Echo-3 Sierra (whom Echo-4 Yankee is fairly sure he asked if paddles were accounted for) left paddles on phone center bank
- Solution: One of us had to reach into the lake to find the line
- Problem: It was dark. Blacker than black. No moon, no stars. Echo-4 Yankee was not afraid to admit he is terrified of the dark. Kept thinking about stories of dead bodies in the lake. Thinking about large eels feasting on dead bodies. Thinking one of those eels might be big enough to pull him in so he might become a dead body
- Solution: Echo-3 Sierra stuck his hand in, found the line, pulled us back to our side of shore
- Problem: Can't sleep thinking about dead bodies on bottom of lake being eaten by eels. Wondering why no one answered phone call. Thinking am alone. Thinking am sad and drunk and cold and lonely and want to go home and what it might be like to be a kidnapped dead girl on the bottom of a lake being eaten by eels

Junkie

SOMETIME IN 2008 THE CORPORAL is lying in a dry canal, waiting for a controlled detonation to submerge his body in sand and overpressure. He can feel dust caking like paste in his eyes and needling into his pores, mixing with the excited sweat on his brow and upper lip. The scrub lining the ground of the wadi rakes and grabs at the corporal's flak jacket, reverberating noise over his tympanum. It sounds like cannons in the paralysis of the moment.

The corporal wonders how he and the lance corporal might explain themselves if they are caught. They are not supposed to be here. They are supposed to be in their trucks. They had to low-crawl from the cordon of the Humvees to avoid detection. How might they explain why they decided to sneak close to the detonation site in order to feel some excitement? Whose idea was it to begin with? The corporal asks these questions, but the lance corporal only shrugs, and smiles, his half-Filipino mocha skin dimpling dark at the cheeks.

Before all the low-crawling and secret squirrel business, they'd kept themselves busy by convincing a private to try to ride a lone cow standing in the fallow field where their platoon had found an ancient cache of rusted mortars, artillery, and RPK rounds. When the private hopped on the bag of bones it bucked like Bodacious and smashed his face, launching him in the air. It must've killed thirty minutes.

In the wadi, the corporal tries recalling the explosive ordnance disposal sergeant's burn scars, which are visible when the sergeant is in his shirtsleeves. The skin is drawn and shining like morning ice spreading on a pond. Sometimes the corporal wishes himself a grievous injury for no better reason than a break in routine.

This deployment has been nothing but routine. No IEDs, no firefights, no ambushes. The corporal still has not killed another human. He kills dogs, and this used to give him satisfaction for days, but now only moments. All they do is find caches and call EOD to blow them up. The low-crawling and threat of danger is the most alive he's felt in months.

He wonders where the intelligence alerting their unit to caches comes from. He wonders how the command decides it's trustable. He wonders if his fiancée is walking to class in West Lafayette, Indiana, at that very moment. He wonders if she's fucking someone else. He wonders what would happen if he won the lottery. He wonders how long it will be before there are colonies on Mars. He wonders why the platoon cares about this desert country, or why any of them think that maybe one day their presence in an unnamed Iraqi village might matter.

The hours of boredom in that field waiting for EOD to blow the cache will become lost hours. What the corporal thought or talked about—whose girlfriends might be cheating on them or who was homesick or who had the best fuck story—will not even settle to the bottom of his gray matter. Its banality will simply vanish from memory forever.

But the minutes in the wadi, waiting for the countdown for the detonation to begin, will remain—like a recollection of catastrophic pain. He knows it was there, that it existed. He will remember the deep marrow-sucking feeling of boredom dissipating, giving way to excitement, danger, exhilaration.

Years later, the corporal will not be able to elicit the month or the day or the hour. In his mind there will be details he might overlay from some other moment: a grove of date palms on the north side of the wadi and more empty fields beyond taken from a different day or year or deployment or life; a sunrise that couldn't have happened because it was already light when he and the lance corporal low-crawled toward the heap of unexploded ordnance; sitting with their backs against crumbling dirt talking about what would come when they were civilians, waiting for the countdown over the comms; a call over the radio ordering all personnel to increase standoff distance because of the amount of UXO—or he might misremember that fact to supplement his fear of their proximity to the blast. The deployment runs together.

He will remember the platoon had already moved to Forward Operating Base Blackhawk on ASR Iron. He remembers FOB Blackhawk was beyond Observation Post Rock and closer to Observation Post Mansion—monolithic remnants of a previous deployment. He will remember how it felt to move back to old stomping grounds and escape Fallujah, the knobs of Humvee tires vibrating through the chassis and frame through his seat as they crossed New Bridge, the Euphrates lazing beneath them fading into the noise of their engines. He will remember Blackwater Bridge to the north and recall a photograph of contractors, burned and hung like meat on display from the green girders. He will remember how the city stopped and peeled into a wide expanse of desert peppered with tiny villages and mud huts and backed-up petrol stops.

He will remember feeling at home making the left turn onto ASR Iron just east of the defunct train trestle, a turn made so many times on a previous deployment. He will remember feeling his face flush and the flesh of his testicles tighten. He will remember telling the Humvee driver to stop the truck as they roll over the culvert that two years before had been packed with one-five-five rounds and propane tanks and whatever other accelerants. He will remember staring at the amoebic concrete patch in the cracked macadam where there used to be a blast crater. He will remember feeling nostalgia and age and sadness that his war was coming to an end.

In the moment, at the bottom of the wadi that cuts through a field in an unnamed Iraqi village just before the controlled cache destruction, he feels none of those things.

In the wadi, the corporal feels young and stupid and is glad for both. He breathes in the dirt as he drags his body behind the lance corporal's, as the soles of the lance corporal's boots push off the corporal's Kevlar helmet, jamming it down his sweat-slick forehead. The short count begins.

The corporal hears the noise and feels the overpressure like being exploded from the inside and compressed from the out all at once. The dust kicks up and the sun shines through beams of filmy mahogany haze. At the bottom of the dry irrigation canal in the unnamed village southwest of Fallujah, which barely shows up on the map, he sees the lance corporal's white teeth against his mauve lips. The look of his smiling mouth solders itself behind the corporal's eyes, and his laugh resonates through muscle and nerve and tendon. He laughs until his abdominals feel like they tear, and rocks and hunks of tough salted earth poke his arms and legs and he'll remember later how fast that moment seemed to pass.

Cold Turkey in Dogwood, Iraq

OVERNIGHT, THE SAND—PULVERIZED TO silt by the tracks of tanks—has hardened, covering the ground with ankle-breaking pocks and craters. We smell like the cheap construction lumber out of which combat engineers built our barracks. It's snowing. We are standing, smoking, not speaking in that quiet snow makes for itself.

Listen up, gents. We're going to Dogwood. We're going to act as a screen for another unit operating to the north. We're tasked with catching squirters. Hey! Put your goddamn cigarette out when I'm talking to you. You'll regret that shit when you're older. One day you'll understand. We're going to Dogwood. Load the trucks, perform inspections, plan to be Oscar Mike in ten. People are watching. We've got to make this look important.

Inside the truck, our spines bend and chests cave, because no matter how much they want us to be boys we don't fit shoulder to shoulder. Our eyes squint and burn against the acrid smoke filling the cabin from pilfered pines. Outside, I know that dogs bark and women cry out to their children but we can't hear them for the engines.

I said I would quit more often than I said I was sorry, so I'm sorry. I try to send the transmission telepathically. I set out that morning, with only one cigarette for the drive and hoped, but knew better, that the distraction of Dogwood might finally help me keep my promise.

I'm awake and everyone nods and bobs. Bobbing for cock, DIs called it in basic. Back when I still wanted to know what it felt like to kill another man. In tiny crimped windows framed by lolling heads I can see my reflection in the perfect black, last cigarette smoldering.

Something in Dogwood's laid the buildings low. Not a one's intact, and I think this might be how the world would look if gods were real and angry. We don't need to use doors to get inside, just lift our legs. But for those watching, we pretend there are walls.

It doesn't take long. The itchy feeling at the base of my skull sends my gloved hand into my hip pocket in search of a fix. A man walks with a metal detector past the ruins of civilization. I know how this place might've looked once, but its fate was to be destroyed over and over. I drop my empty pack in the rubble.

I'm thinking about hoofing hills on Pendleton. Huffing the wild fennel and dusty briny dusk of the Southern California coast and afterward sipping a cold one, the bottle's perspiration sending shivers up my arm. Mountains silhouette themselves in the distance, the lights of barracks rooms like so many fireflies in a field.

On the horizon in Dogwood to our northwest there are no mountains, there are oil refineries in the haze. They are *like* mountains, I think. I could walk there, make it in a few hours. I'd die of thirst before I got halfway. Heat vapors swim past my eyes and I wonder if the snow this morning was a hallucination.

Do you have one, I ask. I ask everyone I know and they all say no. You can't spare one? It's my last. I'd give you mine—no I wouldn't. I'd take a drag, just a puff. I'm saving it for the ride back. I haven't thought about the ride back and I'm coated in dusty dry sweat, left thinking about all the cigarettes I'll never have.

I toe my way through chunks of sand and concrete like an only child on a vacation beach. A crackling voice from the radio attached to my flak jacket is tentative and reports it's found something. I pick up my feet and try to focus.

In movies, bombs beep, they even vibrate—in real life they just explode. I don't hear beeping. There are wires and a rusted artillery shell husk and I push people back. I say, Back up, and call over the radio and don't notice the engineer turn on his metal detector, which begins to beep. My stomach drops and my intestines loosen and my asshole tightens just in time and right then I rethink my promise.

The bomb becomes a shrine. Maybe it knew its destiny at the moment of creation. With its newfound fame come new fresh people who pilgrimage to bring offerings and gifts. A pilgrim offers me cigarettes for unearthing the shrine. When I pay respects with smoke and ash the pilgrims cease to be pilgrims and become explosive ordnance disposal techs. They explode the shrine like it never existed.

Dogwood stinks of concrete and my sweat and ancient desert dust made from the bones and skin of all the people who lived before me. In the whale skeleton of a bombed building, I stare at a bloodstained wall and ash my cigarette in the sand.

The beiges and tans and yellows and grays of Dogwood blend and glob together. I am trying to recall other colors. I remember. I am fifteen, sitting poolside on a warm Indiana night, smoking cigarettes for the first time with a boy I don't like. The tobacco tastes and smells like Midwest summer—chlorine and suntan lotion and baked skin and green. Miles and miles of green.

The unit to our north ends their operation, so we rally. We egress from Dogwood and try to fit together on the road back home. I'm deflated—a Mylar birthday balloon left to tumble on roadsides. Someone snaps a picture and I wonder if there's anything left to develop.

Brothers

WE DON'T ASK. WE DON'T TELL.

We insult and suspect and speculate and then we wrestle and grab ass, feeling one another's hard sinewy bodies beneath our palms while we huff hot breath into one another's ears, whisper sweet nothings, threatening and delivering and dominating.

We sit across from one another and move our callused finger-tips up electric-hard thighs and ask over and over, Are you nervous? Are you nervous? while making an uncomfortable level of eye contact. There is no winning the game. If you get nervous you're a pussy, if you don't, you're a fairy.

We shave hair from our bodies to display thick, veined arms covered in tattoos, sweat beads divide like spermatozoa and chase the contours of our muscles into our palms. While we wait for our turn on the Freedom Bird we pop one another's back zits and apply baby oil to naked shimmering bodies to ensure even tans.

184

In our downtime we gather in shirtless hordes around tiny computer screens to catch a glimpse of money shots spurting from gargantuan cocks while we strain against the crotches of our trousers. We retreat to the showers, relieve the tension, and return for more.

We call this brotherhood.

You're all a bunch of queers, says an outsider.

Spartans fucked each other all the time, we say.

You fight harder for someone you love, we say.

Don't you want to be loved? we ask.

What happens in the field stays in the field, we say.

I'd let Brad Pitt fuck me in the ass, one of us says.

Let him, another says. Like he'd come around asking.

We say these things for shock, for a laugh, but there is truth to them. There are reasons for their recurrence. We are trying to figure it out, trying to find ourselves in a world of testosterone and violence, a world where there is little room for love and tenderness. So we throw around faggot and queer and poke fun at the effeminate because we've learned to fear those intimate feelings, those intense moments of love that swell inside us.

Guys, one of us says. I'm gay.

We know, we say. We've always known.

And maybe we have known, and maybe we haven't, but in that moment it does not matter. In that moment we are reflecting on all the things we have said and done and all the ways we have insulted him and all the times he has kept quiet. We are ashamed to have treated one of our own this way. He has sweated with us and lost with us and bled with us and we are all the same inhuman things now, unloved and unwanted and cast again and again into the desert. We think about this and we understand that he has been cast further than us, that he has been struggling and sinking in the desert sands for years alone and it is because of us. We enfold him and defend him and love him like brothers.

Mt. Marine Corps

A good metaphor for the Marine Corps is to think of the organization like it is a mountain.

But it's a mountain with many false peaks.

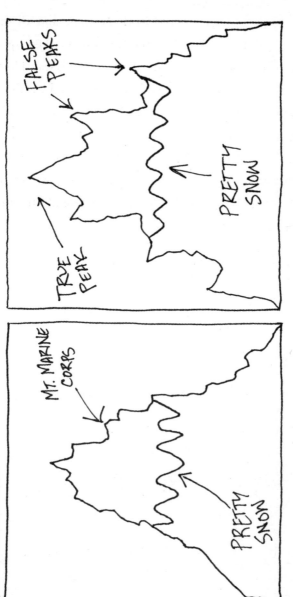

At the true peak, there's one person in charge, but at every different false peak there's also a person who is in charge and who thinks they live at the top.

Then at the base of the mountain there is us, the junior enlisted. We stare up at the mountain and dream of life on one of the peaks.

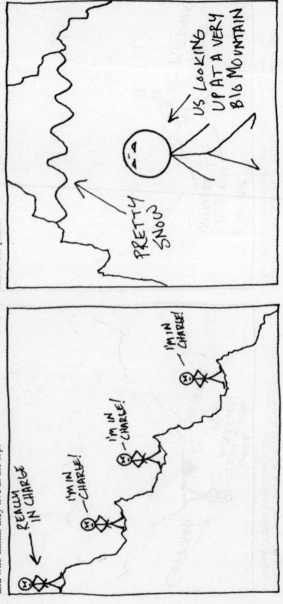

REALLY IN CHARGE

I'M IN CHARGE!

I'M IN CHARGE!

I'M IN CHARGE!

PRETTY SNOW

US LOOKING UP AT A VERY BIG MOUNTAIN

One problem with the metaphorical mountain is the conundrum of what to do with the metaphorical shit. Where to dispose of those bothersome turds?

Command could walk down to the base to evacuate the metaphorical shit, dispose of it properly—but it is below their station. Easier to shit over the side and let gravity sort it out.

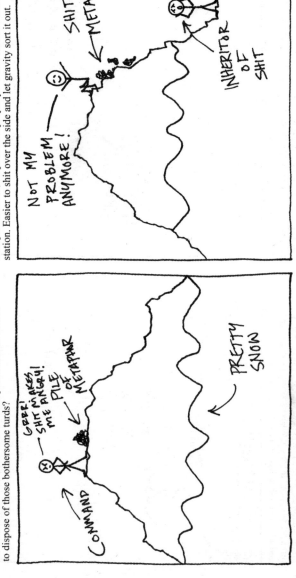

When the shit rolls downhill, everyone who thought they were in charge gets reminded they aren't and they get mad and send the shit even farther downhill, with their own shit added on. This is a cumulative process.

The metaphorical shit accumulates and rolls, picking up all the detritus in its path until it reaches us at the base and crashes like a giant shit tsunami.

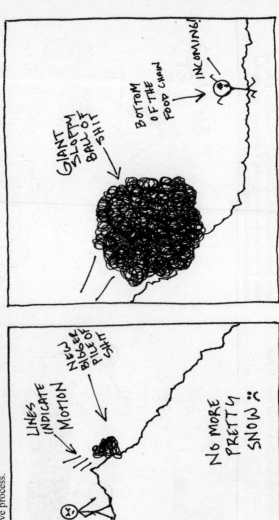

We end up covered in stinking metaphorical shit. It becomes our problem to deal with through no fault of our own . . . most of the time.

But sometimes we get covered in our own shit. We think we're getting one over on Command by sneaking to the top of the mountain and leaving a huge steaming metaphorical dump right on their doorstep.

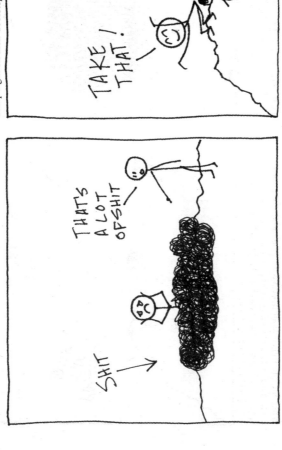

In our excitement, we forget that the metaphorical shit will roll downhill. That it is an irregular, foreign shit makes everyone want to know where it came from. The people on the way have a choice: find whoever was responsible, or take the blame.

Our metaphorical shit is a video of us dancing on the hood of a truck while it rolls down a road in Ferris Town—an apartment community south of Fallujah—posted to the internet. In 2006 we had to run between the buildings in Ferris Town because of snipers. It isn't like that in 2008.

The video makes Command look like they don't have any situational awareness, like they are incompetent, that they are the reason the war has lost public approval.

Command interrogates us, seizes our electronics. They know who made the video, but they want to know whether or not we were all complicit. It only takes one to break.

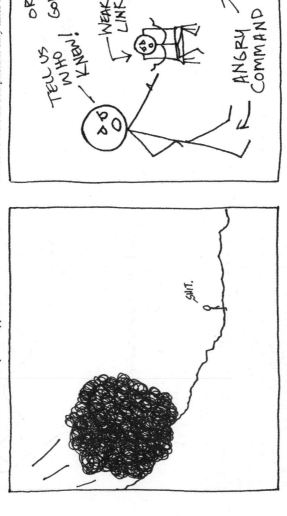

Command just wants the video to disappear, but the glory of the internet is forever and even though we are disbanded and our rank is taken, our contracts only last four years and they are almost up. Because of the internet and some serious dance moves, we managed to leave some shit at the top of the mountain. Sometimes, people ask us if it was worth it. Eat the apple, fuck the Corps, we say. Only that it makes a good story.

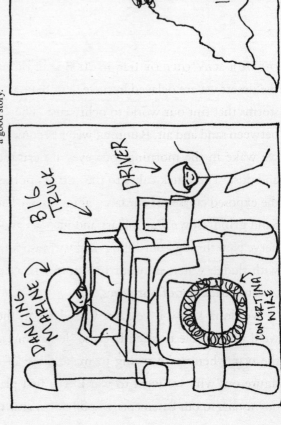

Clean

ON OUR WAY OUT OF Iraq in 2008 after our second pump to the desert we are delayed by a week of shamal winds and sand-storms that tint our world to ochre rust. There is no difference between sand and air. Running water becomes pointless. When we wake in the mornings our eyes are crusted shut by saline and dust. The muck cakes to the corners of our mouths, stains the exposed creases of our faces, aging us like bad stage makeup. Sand grinds down our molars and incisors and sends tinges of nerve pain through our fillings and we wash it down our gullets with sludge water, into our intestines where it's absorbed and sweated back out of our pores.

We don't know it yet, but years later in the dead of night we'll not be able to sleep because sleep won't come easy after the war when we're trying to make sense of it all, trying to figure out why we went to war in the first place. We'll sneak downstairs to our basements, or pull down attic doors and wince at the creaking echo of wood on metal, or we'll tiptoe to our garages or sheds or forgotten closets and sift through boxes of Christmas and Halloween decorations until we find a pilfered olive drab ruck or decaying cardboard box or thick plastic foot-locker. We'll run our hands over its surface, gooseflesh rising on our arms.

Inside we'll find that dust in crumpled seabags and in the pockets of old utilities and creases of stolen gear. It will stink of eons, a stale flat stink that will leave our mouths dry and our throats looking like the parched hardpan on which we used to piss. Finding the sand is like stumbling upon old nude photos of an ex and as our groins stir to life we'll look over our guilty shoulders for our wives and girlfriends and partners. We'll rub the grit between our forefingers and thumbs, the grains echoing like artillery against the deltas and islands of our fingerprints. Our hearts will race and we'll stand inside our warm domestic houses remembering the thing we used to be in the desert, and we'll know we won't ever be able to leave the thing or the desert behind.

Long hairs on our scalps will trap the grime, which will powder our eyelashes and stick to our nose hairs, and will seep over us like a spilled shadow, curling around us like a cat's tail.

We'll pack the trinkets up and we'll sneak to our bathrooms to shower and remove any evidence of our indiscretion, our wives and partners still dozing. The dust will leach red and thick from our bodies and spread to the chlorinated water collecting at our toes like blood trails from a shark bite.

Some of us will shave our heads right there in the bathroom, thinking the dust is an infestation like lice. Thinking maybe we can get at it without our obstructing forest of hair. We'll scrub and scrub and grate and rake and we'll slough off dead dogs and detained children and widowed women. They'll collect around our soaking legs and we'll beg their lifeless and horrified eyes for forgiveness but they'll already be circling the drain.

Out of the tub, skin steaming, noses full of potpourri and feminine soaps, we'll stand in front of the fogged mirror, suck in slack hairy paunches, slap lobstered flesh, and remember when we could bench-press more than our own weight and run three miles in eighteen minutes.

We'll remember the times we overpowered one another in the dirt after flak jacket runs and how we fireman-carried the weak during battalion hikes through sunbaked hills. We'll think of the boy in basic training who pissed his trousers, and the stench of barracks rooms full of molded low-pile carpet and Pledge surface cleaner, and the hair dryer feeling of being in a Humvee turret behind an Abrams. Our faces will flush at the thought of our own disappointments, our own missed chances, our ignorance, our cruelty.

Then we'll slide back into bed under our six-hundred-thread-count sheets and our floral print duvets next to whomever and stare at the ceiling hoping and praying that none of the dust remains, but also hoping we missed some crevice, some fold of skin. Thinking that maybe if we wash it all away we might finally be able to get a decent goddamn night of sleep, but afraid that if and when we do rid ourselves of the chaff that we might disappear ourselves, be washed down the drain, our skin and sinew and bones sliding into the blackness.

Self-Diagnosis: Sick of Running

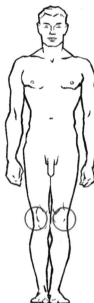
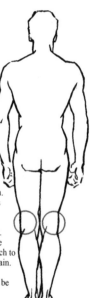

Patient complains of
phantasmic knee pain.
Pain not *in* his knees
but in his *knees*, the
place beyond his
knees, between body
and soul, and
everyone knows
a grunt's soul resides
in the knees.
Patient wants to start
over. Wants to leave
old knees behind,
build new knees.
Thinks: maybe in
new life will not have
to run any longer.
Thinks: maybe
can finally tell the truth.
About everything. This
scares patient. Patient
scared to start again.
Means leaving comfort.
Means will have to face
unknown again. So much to
know. Means trying again.
Means being human.
Patient inquires how to be
human. Patient asks,
How to be real?

How to Throw a Drunken Punch

THINK ABOUT THE TWENTY-SEVEN BONES that make up your hand. The phalanges, the metacarpals, the carpus—not to mention your radius and ulna, which, while bones technically making up your forearm, are impacted nonetheless by throwing a punch. And now think about a face. Fourteen bones—nasal bone, zygomatic bone, maxilla, mandible, what have you. You know the words because those are the bones that shattered in Keene Sherburne's face in Iraq in 2006 when your Humvee rolled over a few hundred pounds of explosives packed into a drainage culvert. Remember the feel of Keene's spongy rippling skin as the ocean of bone moved below. In any other world twenty-seven against fourteen are good odds. Not in the world of bones.

Now, think about your hand and where you want the punch to connect. See your target, then try to see through it to the dartboard or jukebox or whatever else is behind your target and visualize your punch driving through your target and hitting that thing. Your offhanded leg should be forward, your dominant leg back. So when you throw the punch it will birth itself at your strong heel. The labor should be forceful enough to send a wave of screaming, targeted energy through your body. The punch will shimmy its way on up through your strong leg. A leg that is powerful from running and humping the coastal hills of Camp Pendleton, through shit fields in the Euphrates River Valley, across endless deserts. This will happen like lightning; the delivery pains of the punch last fractions of seconds. It will travel through your lower back and up your latissimus dorsi and into your rear deltoids, and then it will slam itself from strong-side front deltoid to bicep, forcing the muscles to extend, turning your forearm into a whip-and-maul mechanism.

Your target is not the man; it is not even the thing behind the man. Your target is a feeling—of life of living of fear of control. How do you explain a feeling? You don't know, except when you find it. And you've often found it through punching.

The punch connects.

But has it connected true? Have you followed the movements of throwing a punch? If so, see figure 1. However, if you've been drinking, which you have, see figures 2 and 3.

VICTORY!

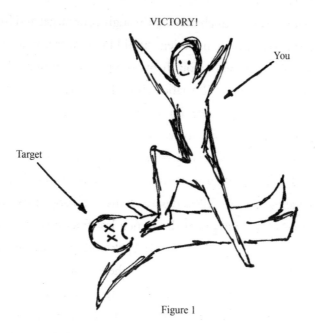

Target

You

Figure 1

In all likelihood, you have not thought about the previous things because you are drunk. So the rules of throwing a punch are out. You have instead thrown a drunken punch—a punch that should have never been born, a punch that should have been aborted, and it makes its way into the world looking like something that has been. There are no rules for the drunken punch, only for the inevitable that follows.

The punch originated not in your heel, but in your mind. It looked fantastic and heroic and lovely and you imagined the blow jobs and fucking it would garner you. You picture women lined up around the globe in awe of your punching prowess, your compatriots hoisting you above their heads and praising you as their leader. In your mind you saw those things when you should have seen the target. And so this was the result of your punch:

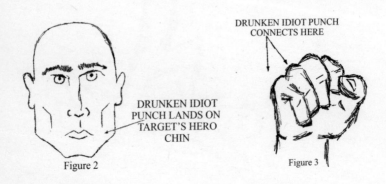

DRUNKEN IDIOT PUNCH
CONNECTS HERE

DRUNKEN IDIOT
PUNCH LANDS ON
TARGET'S HERO
CHIN

Figure 2

Figure 3

Here we are again with bones. You've landed on the largest of his and the smallest of yours. It is a VW Beetle running headlong into a Mack truck. At the moment of impact your delusions burst into bone shards.

Now observe the sudden movement of your former target's heel, the slight telegraphing of his fist, the pullback, which warns you you're about to be punched. Know that this is good, the telegraphing, it takes away a few pounds of power behind the punch. Imagine all those women who will spit on you now instead of blowing you, and your friends who will leave you bloodied on the floor, and your family whom you've disappointed. Notice a slice of yellow incandescent light escaping the open entry, cutting a wedge onto the inky pavement in the Southern California darkness. Wish to be out there, beyond the light in a place where bones might not matter. Forget the pain in your hand and try not to think about the inevitable rain of blows to come.

Think about where this all went wrong.

Cause and Effect

Dear Past-me,

At this moment in time, August 2008, you are skidding off *Cristianitos Road in the passenger seat of Chris's Toyota Tacoma as you and Chris return from day drinking at San Onofre Beach so you can continue drinking at the barracks. The Tacoma is screeching to the north side of the road, but soon it will hit dirt and sand and rocks, in turn blowing out the passenger-side tires and causing the truck to barrel-roll—twice—as you'll learn later from the friend (whose name you'll not be able to recall six years from now) driving behind you.*

You've been stateside from your second Iraq deployment for three months, and so it has been three months of nightly drinking: thirty-packs of Yellow Bellies, fifths of whiskey, bottles of red wine, Grey Goose vodka on the rocks, and then well vodka straight.

This day, of the ten or so people at the beach, six of you drank a half gallon of whiskey. You turned it into a game: Ring of Fire. The cap came off, got tossed in the flames, and everyone passed the bottle

206

until the booze was gone. Willy T. finished off the last half inch in a single chug and retched into the fire, which ignited the alcohol vomit and turned Willy T. into a human flamethrower.

After that, Willy T. asked for a ride home.

People offered to drive you and Chris, but Chris said he was fine.

And now the crash is happening. The crash is happening not because you are both drunk, but because you decided to change shirts. A decision, which seemed logical at the time, because you're going to hit the PX for more beer and 1) you don't want to catch shit for wearing inappropriate clothing in the PX and 2) you've decided the cutoff shirt you're currently wearing makes you look like a disgusting slob. A viewpoint, which can be traced to body dysmorphia established in your youth by bullying, poor diet, lack of exercise, etc., and is only made worse by the drinking. You change your shirt, unbuckling your seat belt to do so, and Chris decides to teach you a lesson in safety by swerving the wheel back and forth.

From here your lives will take different paths.

In the aftermath, Chris will get busted. He will not be allowed to deploy to Iraq as you had both volunteered to do. He'll get an on-base DUI, which in the long run won't matter because of the military sovereignty of Camp Pendleton. While you're gone, he will get busted again, this time for possession of controlled substances—marijuana and anabolic steroids. He will do brig time and then later be restricted to his (your) barracks room. Later, he will work as a bouncer at bars in Dana Point and get offered a job working for a high-powered client. He will go on to make large sums of money and find a girl in

Southern California. He will have business ideas about marketing survival gear to the unprepared. He will marry the girl from Southern California. He will style himself as an alternative personal trainer complete with his own brand of outdoors workout regimen. He will be successful and independent and from time to time he will send you a text message if something in his life reminds him of you. He will make time to come to your wedding.

Meanwhile, you will still deploy, because Chris will save you. When the friend-whose-name-you-won't-remember's car stops, Chris will direct a dazed and drunken you into that car. You will not protest. Six years later you will not be sure of all these details. You will not be sure you were conscious the whole time, nor will you be sure of how you ended up in the space between dashboard and window. Or how you lived. But you will still deploy because you will not be in Chris's truck when it shambles past the office of the officer on duty, and so Chris has saved you.

He will go on to continually save you. When you return from deployment, he will save you from bar fights and from choking on your own vomit as you sleep and from all the weakness and cowardice that lives inside of you, because he's always been the strong one and you've always relied on him to buttress your fragility.

The truck has hit the sandy shoulder. It is flipping down an embankment into the wild fennel and scrub and loose sand. You are bouncing around the single cab of the Tacoma like so many lottery balls. Later you will think of Keene and the culvert bomb that wrecked his face and scrambled both your brains. This is like that except that it's not. Not exactly.

In the moments after the crash, you will think everything will be fine. You will think that it's a good time to stop drinking. You will think about calling your mother—your father, even. You will think that life is short and it is stupid to do things to make it shorter. You will think about atoning and healing and living a good life, how you could maybe start living a good life.

But of course you will do none of those things you think about, because you are weak, and you are a coward, and those are things Chris can't control.

Past-me, I'm happy you can't read this letter. Because if you could you might change. I'm glad not to be able to tell you to stand by your friend and deal with the consequences and not get in Friend-Whose-Name-I-Can't-Remember's car. If you were able to do that, you might avoid everything coming your way. And that wouldn't be fair, because you deserve it all. You deserve the twisted metal and horrible aftermath. You deserve to tumble and twist through the air for eternity—one day you'll see that.

Love,

Me

The Wizard

THE WIZARD IS AWARE OF his reputation. He knows what the young Marines ordered to see him think of him. He knows they call him the Wizard—a roundabout reference to needing a brain. He knows they think of him as the enemy, that they lie to him more often than tell the truth, that their senior enlisted commanders tell them if they fail a psych evaluation they'll receive dishonorable discharges, be branded failures, cowards, be thrown in mental institutions.

How are things going back in Indiana? What does your family think of you volunteering to go back to Iraq? asks the Wizard, who smiles at the surprise on the Marine's face at the word Indiana.

You know, not bad, says the Marine shifting his weight in the chair. They're proud of me.

Not bad might be the most truthful statement he'll get out of this Marine. The Wizard tries to decide what not bad might mean on a graded scale. Is it better than bad? Probably. But is it worse than good? Is it worse than okay? He decides it sits somewhere around the former.

The Marine's name tape above his right breast pocket reads YOUNG. There is no irony in the name. The boy in front of the Wizard is twenty-two. He's only been able to vote in one presidential election. He looks like he might need to shave every other day at most. Still, the Wizard knows twenty-two is ancient in the Marines. In the infantry the boy is dust.

How many drinks would you say you've had in the past week? None, one to two, three to five, six or more? the Wizard asks.

One. Maybe two, says the Marine.

The Wizard smells the yeasty booze stink from the previous night seeping from the Marine's skin. There are mouth-shaped bruises low on his neck.

Have a girlfriend back in Indiana? asks the Wizard. It is not a question on the pre-deployment health assessment checklist, but he feels an opening after not bad and so tries his luck.

A fiancée, sir.

The Wizard flinches at sir. The Marine has doubled down, reset the boundaries between enlisted and officer. The Wizard nods, flips some pages in the Marine's medical record—standard fare aside from an IED blast in 2006. There were most likely other unreported minor incidents as well. The Wizard knows that platoon corpsmen treat the Marines without entering information at the aid station—ingrown toenails, sicknesses, lacerations, contusions, minor concussions from things no one wants to explain. He knows the corpsmen give the Marines Ativan when they cannot sleep and he knows the corpsmen provide the Marines with intravenous saline when the Marines drink too much. This is standard practice to keep information out of medical records, to keep the Marines from being accused of malingering, to keep the Marines with their companies and platoons—their families. The Wizard knows this, but it does not make him happy.

Do you ever have lingering thoughts, dreams, or nightmares about your time in Iraq? asks the Wizard, changing the subject, trying to catch the Marine off guard.

Oh no, sir, says the Marine. No nightmares. Never, sir.

The Marine could be telling the truth. It is not out of the ordinary for Marines to not have nightmares. The Wizard knows there are other ways to treat trauma besides pills and therapy. He knows distance runners, statistically, experience trauma to a lesser degree than non-runners. This Marine does not look like a distance runner. This Marine looks bloated from alcohol and his fingers are stained yellow by nicotine. His eyes are bloodshot and his hair must be beyond the regulation three inches.

Do you use tobacco products—cigarettes, cigars, pipe, hookah, dip, chew, snuff—any of them? asks the Wizard.

I quit smoking after my second deployment, sir, says the Marine.

The Wizard's eyes go to the rectangular outline of a cigarette pack in the Marine's trousers pocket, and now he wants to jump from his chair and grab the Marine by his collar and scream in his face, I am trying to help you, asshole! Just tell me the truth!

The Wizard smiles. Good, he says. Very good.

He notices the Marine's knuckles. They are scarred and scabbed, misshapen.

Do you ever feel yourself becoming angry for no reason? asks the Wizard.

No, sir, says the Marine.

He does not blame the Marine for lying. If the Marine were to confess his drinking habits and familial issues and nightmares and tell the stories of the road map of knuckle scars, the Wizard would not deem him fit for deployment. But if the Marine were to confess those things, the Wizard might be able to help—with the drinking the rage the compulsive lying.

One last question, says the Wizard. Why did you volunteer to return to Iraq?

The Marine pauses; perspiration pops on his forehead. The Wizard wills the Marine to tell him the truth, to spill his pickled guts all over the desk between them, to collapse in a sweaty tearful pile and beg for help. The Wizard would hold the Marine, he would stroke his hair and shush him and sing him lullabies. Tell me, thinks the Wizard. I know you want to, just do it, come on, tell me everything.

To defend my country and its people, sir, says the Marine.

The Wizard nods, the sound of his pen looping the arcs of his name as he signs his approval like nails on a chalkboard in his ears. He smiles at the Marine and hands over the paper.

Next! he calls, watching the Marine walk past a line of other Marines getting their stories square while they wait.

Third Time's the Charm

IN SEPTEMBER 2008, WE RETURN to Iraq as volunteers to augment the regimental commander's security detail. Instead of holes in the sand covered by camouflaged netting there are temperature-controlled trailers with bunk beds and mattresses. Instead of jerking off to the same cache of porn we have access to the Internet and the possibilities are endless. Instead of MREs or the occasional breakfast meal brought to a rooftop lookout by a hospitable farmer there's a mess hall open from four in the morning until midnight. There's a Burger King. A no-shit, real, honest-to-god Burger King that sells Whoppers. Instead of trash cans filled with sun-boiled giardia-filled water there's an Olympic-sized pool spoken of in hushed tones, as if the acknowledgment of its existence might cause the water to spontaneously evaporate, leaving behind only chalky chlorine residue on Persian blue tile. Even as we buoy in the chemicals, red-rimmed eyes stinging, we wait for indirect fire or sniper potshots or to be called up for quick reaction force. Real gymnasiums replace the relics once created from tent poles and cinder blocks and sandbags at commandeered houses. Now the weights are made of iron and rubber and feel foreign in our callus-covered hands.

There are no more patrols, no more explosions, no more raids. There are police actions, there is winning hearts and minds, there is peacetime and domestication.

We try to resist domestication, hold to our unbroken stallion nature. But we're really not much more than feral dogs at heart—swayed by the promise of sturdy roofs and hot chow.

There's not much fight left in us.

There are no more tactical firing ranges, no more sun-bleached camouflage utilities, no bloodstains, no mud, no detainees. No more John Wayne.

Instead, we are taught sword manual and drill manual and even though we are deployed in a war zone our cammies stay stark and new and never fade. The bills of our covers parallel the bridges of our noses and our diaphragms work double time. We march one another back and forth across a sandy parade deck marked by engineer tape—the same way we used to mark out complex floor plans to teach impromptu classes on close quarters battle.

Now we give hip-pocket lessons on Marine Corps customs and courtesies and grooming standards. We inspect one another for uniform discrepancies. We fill out bubbles on Scantron tests and sit in air-conditioned classrooms in tent cities congratulating one another on how well we've learned to be Marines when the results come back.

In the end, we tried for so long, clawed tooth and nail, and swallowed our pride to get back to our war, that we didn't realize it had already ended.

Trajectory

IN EARLY 2009 I AM tasked to hold security on an Iraqi man sedated on a hospital bed. I've just left him, replaced by the next guard. The man was shot in the left calf, but the bullet exited close to his abdomen—I am amazed by this. The elephantine swelling caused by the wound fascinates me. To relieve pressure the doctors cut the man's skin to the muscle. They do not explain to me why they had to relieve the pressure this way, but it leaves the inner workings of the man's striated sinew exposed, pink and glossy and hard to look at but impossible not to. Sometimes the nurses let me flush and loosely redress the wound. Sometimes I press just a bit too hard or am careless about where my fingers make contact. There is a part of me that wants to see the man suffer. I have been told he was shot because he was also shooting, though his bullets didn't strike true.

Bullets are tricky. They don't travel in the straight lines movies make them out to. Bullets move in a parabolic free fall.

They begin to tumble, asteroids in space, toward their point of impact to do whatever damage.

Small caliber bullets, like a 5.56mm ball round from an M16 or M4, are not made to travel through bodies and leave an exit wound. Rounds fired from an M16A4 service rifle travel at 3,110 feet per second, but even at close range a 5.56 might not make it all the way through a person. The bullet will start to tumble through the viscera and fracture bones and make secondary fragmentation within the target's body, and it might enter the chest or the abdomen or the face, but it might end up exiting through the kneecap or the elbow or the buttock. Both holes might be small, but internally it will look like someone eggbeatered the organs.

A human can't act on a bullet once the bullet has entered the human; there is too much velocity, too much power. Most times the human doesn't even know the bullet has entered them until it has exited or become lodged somewhere against some dense bone or within thick tissue.

I have acted like a bullet. I entered lives and bounced and ricocheted and broke and tore. Now I am going to exit one life and that life will have no say.

Unlike the bullet, I am exiting by choice, not because of ballistics. I am exiting because I have lied and cheated and now that I am sober I realize those things are not foundational to lifelong bonds of marriage.

I will exit ten thousand klicks away via international phone line, because I am a coward, because I didn't have the courage to tell the truth to her face two months before with the Pacific coast of California as my backdrop. In that moment I was still somehow tricking both of us that I loved her.

I expect the conversation will be long and I am thinking of the collateral damage of my exit.

There are four weapons-safety rules Marines learn in basic training:

1. Treat every weapon as if it were loaded.
2. Never point a weapon at anything you do not intend to shoot.
3. Keep your finger straight and off the trigger until you are ready to fire.
4. Keep your weapon on safe until you intend to fire.

There is also an unspoken fifth among grunts: Know your target and what lies beyond. I am thinking about what I might hit upon my exit after these four years, how many relationships I am changing the course of. How many people won't have control of that fallout, just like the person in the next room can't control the bullet exiting the first body, traveling through drywall or stucco, and striking them.

I am in an AT&T phone trailer. The trailer is empty, for which I'm grateful. I use a calling card to phone.

Hello?
Hey, it's me.

Hi! How are you doing? What time is it there?

Early. Listen. I think we should talk.

[Silence]

I just don't think this is working. I feel like I'm wasting your
    time. I am not a good person.

You don't mean that. What's going on?

Nothing. This isn't working. It's over. I'm sorry.

[Phone clicks]

That's it. Is that it? She was crying. How can that be it? No
screaming, no fuck you. Clean. Surgical.

Back in the aid station the Iraqi man is gone; well enough to
travel, he was taken by the men who shot him to be interrogated at some other base somewhere. Maybe he'll be impris-
oned. Maybe he'll be set free. I knew nothing about him, only
that he was reported to have fired a weapon at soldiers and I
was to guard him and that because of him my sleep was interrupted and so I hated him.

The bed is spotless, sheets bright and starched and empty.
And I start to feel like my bones are collapsing from the inside
out, like I'm being eviscerated. I start to cry. I want to apologize to the man. I want to tell him I'm sorry for how I treated
him, for not protecting him when that was the job I was
assigned to. But the man is gone, and all that's left is an exit
wound.

Chewing the Fat

WE HAVE LEARNED THE LESSON to work smarter not harder over the past three and a half years. So instead of cherry pickers and steam engines and mountain climbers and side straddle hops and push-ups and crunches and running we order steroids.

We consult with a friend back home via instant messaging from our air-conditioned four-man trailer. Where do we get them? What do we want to get? Orals? Injectables? How long should we take them? How much at one time? Side effects? Concerns?

We want to take them because we spend chunks of time in the gym. We want to take them because we feel our bodies getting older, worn-out from living in our gear and riding hunched over in Humvees and getting exploded and dodging bullets and living in fear and coping with drink. We want to take them to get strong, to see more gains from our lifting. We want to take them to look like the way we think we're supposed to look for the Corps for our families and our girlfriends and wives or boyfriends or whatever. We want to take them to look good naked.

Mostly, like all other things we do, we do them because we are bored and we want to pass the time.

With research we find Japan is our answer. Japan, where our path should've taken us what seems like all those years ago. We imagine Okinawan soapies we never got, the Jungle Warfare Training Center we were never a part of (though we probably would've bitched the whole time anyhow), the cammies and school shirts we never traded with Filipino Marines, the balloons held over our heads that were never popped by the atom-spearing tip of a dart shot from the vagina of a Thai stripper. All of these things zip through our minds as we peruse the clean, medical-looking Japanese website. Test 250, *add to cart*. Winstrol 100, *add to cart*.

The six-by-nine bubble mailer arrives during mail call some weeks later. Our staff sergeant hands us the package. There is Japanese writing on the label. In our trailer we tear at the packing tape, sliding our fingertips over the kanji. We stash the juice in a pair of new boots reserved for our plane ride home.

We approach a corpsman we call Hang Ten Tony, in hopes that he might procure for us retractable syringes—enough for our twelve-week cycle. And he does. Between Hang Ten Tony and the Navy there is no loss of love. Hang Ten Tony misses his surfboard and his weed and not taking orders from dickhead Marines. Hang Ten Tony wants to fuck the system as much as we do. So he helps us. He shows us where to inject the drugs into our muscle groups, and how to avoid nerve strikes. He monitors our injection points and keeps us as sterile as possible.

We become supplicants of the iron and cable, we shun cardio, we eat as clean as we can—eggs, oatmeal, almonds, chicken, chicken, chicken, vegetables, chicken, oatmeal, eggs, chicken, almonds. Our glutes grow sore to the touch. Hang Ten Tony advises us to switch cheeks and shoot into the left. We shoot into quads and into pecs and delts.

There are gains, but not like we thought. Hang Ten Tony has no thoughts as to why—he is a specimen, a swimmer and surfer and marathon runner, his body would make Renaissance sculptors swoon.

We grow bulky with water weight. We get stronger, though not as strong as we would like. We must be doing something wrong.

We ask around casually and hear stories of friends of friends of other Marines who ordered juice from overseas only to find later they had been injecting rooster semen. Our steroids do not look like rooster semen. But we do wonder. There is no roid rage, no mood swings. Mostly, we are calm and collected. And that also makes us suspicious.

The cycle ends. The steroids are gone. Without the steroids we begin to ask, what is the point? Why do we give a fuck about looking good naked? Why were we ever crazy enough to stick ourselves with needles in the first place? We want to go back to how we were, when we used to rely on our rank and charm to keep us out of trouble. We want to say, Eat the apple, fuck the Corps.

But still, we are in the gym every morning, and when the time comes to cut weight, in the afternoons we run. We log miles, sometimes we sprint intervals. And the entire time we are asking one another and ourselves, why continue?

We sweat and we hurt and our lungs burn and our muscles ache, and we question. We are learning, and we are cutting. We are cutting more than water weight, more than fat. We are cutting baggage. We are cutting what made us heavy. We do the thing now just to do the thing. Because we get pleasure out of breathing so heavy our throats bleed. As we sprint intervals and squat ass to the grass and push weights from our chests, the three years behind us stand in front of our eyes like a movie we can't look away from. We see the entire time we were looking for a way to game the game, to beat the system, to work smarter not harder. We thought if we didn't move no one would see us, but the more we stayed still the more time slowed. We see our past weakness and we shove back stronger. The faster we sprint, the deeper we squat, the harder we push, the more we move, the faster time begins to flow, and the more we begin to worry about the future.

A Moment of Clarity

Hang Ten Tony's Apartment

HANG TEN TONY IS TALL, heavily muscled, tanned, blond. Hang Ten Tony has a gap in his front teeth, which are paper white. It is an endearing gap, a gap I want to see, a gap I could fall through for eternity. Freckled sunspots dot his nose. Hang Ten Tony is talking to me about surfing, about how good it is to be home, about hating the Navy. Hang Ten Tony is taking bong rips and drinking a cerveza, bro.

Now Hang Ten Tony is talking about starting a business, about skipping to Mexico, about marrying a girl in Hawaii on top of an active volcano. I try to tell Hang Ten Tony that relationships are hard, but he does not hear me. Hang Ten Tony is pacing and manic and I am uncomfortable. I am wishing I had ignored his call. Hang Ten Tony cashes out the bong, drips

Visine into his eyeballs, and pops an Altoid or two into his mouth.

Hang Ten Tony says it's time to go.

Hang Ten Tony on How to Stay Hydrated

Every morning, bro, I'm telling you, eight ounces of water right when you wake up does so much for your health. And it's all about your health, bro, you know? I mean, if you don't have your health what do you really got?

At this moment, Hang Ten Tony is plunging a needle attached to a syringe full of testosterone into my right buttock.

And coffee, too, you know? You want to get a little bit of that caffeine in your system. Some water and then some coffee, they'll both work to stimulate your metabolism so you'll burn more calories throughout the day.

My muscle feels distended and thick like an overcooked steak. I nod and say things like, For sure, and, Right on, and, Most definitely. They feel strange as they travel over my lips.

All right, bro. This is about where you're going to want the injection site to be. Just take your thumb and pinkie—yeah like that, like the mellow sign, bro. And put your thumb on your hipbone and your pinkie at about a forty-five degree angle and then, bam. That's where you go. Cool? And remember bro, water, a little bit of coffee, get hydrated, jump-start that metabolism early in the morning.

Hang Ten Tony on the Way to El Toro

Hang Ten Tony and I are driving to El Toro to meet Hang Ten Tony's friend and his friend's fiancée. Hang Ten Tony's friend is in his twenties and still lives with his parents and attends Irvine Valley College. The house is located just off the Five but deep in a residential neighborhood where I lose all sense of direction for the lack of colors other than taupe, beige, khaki, and desert pink.

Hang Ten Tony commandeers the radio, plays loud music I don't know, and then lights a huge joint. Hang Ten Tony yells at me over the music. He talks more about getting married in Hawaii on top of an active volcano.

So, like, my family and her family will just wait at the base of the volcano or whatever, and then, like, a helicopter will take her and me to the top and land for, like, fifteen or twenty minutes so we can do the ceremony, he says.

Wow, yeah that's pretty—

But, bro, that's not even it! It'll come pick us up and then drop us back down with everyone else.

What about the officiator?

The what, bro?

Whoever's going to marry you.

Oh man, helicopter pilots can do that.

228

I think you're thinking of ship captains.

Maybe them, too, but definitely helicopter pilots.

Hang Ten Tony and After Hours Karaoke at a Sushi Bar

Onstage, Hang Ten Tony's knuckles turn white as he clutches the microphone. The place is empty aside from Hang Ten Tony's friend, his friend's fiancée, and three drunk sushi chefs, who are cheering on Hang Ten Tony as he sings a sweaty and tone-deaf version of "Sweet Dreams" by the Eurythmics.

So is Anthony going to be okay? He seems different, says Friend's Fiancée.

He's been gone a year—I didn't hook up with them over there until six months ago. A year is a long time, I say.

This just isn't him, you know? says Friend.

No, I guess I don't, I say.

Well, like, I've never seen him drunk before, says Friend.

We all turn to look at Hang Ten Tony. The sushi chefs are onstage with him now. He is lifting them up and air humping them and they are all laughing.

Was this your first time in Iraq? Friend's Fiancée asks. She pronounces it E-rock.

Third, I say.

Hang Ten Tony's friend and his friend's fiancée exchange looks. I am painfully aware of the look. Their look says, Oh my god. This person might snap at any moment. Look what this person has turned our friend into. This person is a monster. We pity monsters.

I want to say I am not damaged. I want to say I am not a monster. But instead I say, I didn't even get to kill anyone.

I can tell they linger on the word get and I down the rest of my beer, turning back to Hang Ten Tony as he ends his performance.

Hang Ten Tony's friend and his friend's fiancée leave soon after the look and forget about me. That night I cannot sleep.

Hang Ten Tony on a Night Patrol

There is no light pollution in Iraq. There might've been once, but not anymore. Bombs dropped, buildings collapsed, people died. But now there are stars. More stars than I will ever see again in my life.

This is the good thing about being a turret gunner. I am in the truck, but I am also not. I am safe, but I am autonomous. I can be alone. I can think. I can feel the winter-crisp desert air numbing my face. It is clean, somehow lighter. It is January. I have less than two weeks left in country and less than ninety days on my military contract. And then I will be a civilian again.

I scan the utter dark for anything unusual, any movement, as I've been trained to do. I think that this will be one of the last times I will do this, and a wave of melancholy washes over me. I know this, I think. What else do I know?

The convoy stops for a security halt.

Man, fuck this, says Hang Ten Tony from inside the cab.

It's not so bad, I say. It's not so bad.

Missed Connection

Dear San Clemente Cabbie,

You picked up my brother, my uncle, and me from a strip bar named Captain Cream's in El Toro, California, and drove us back to San Clemente in early 2009. Do you remember that night in January, Cabbie? You must. How could you not? If you didn't remember, it would suggest that kind of thing happens to you often, and if that's the case I advise a change in profession—not that you're to blame for my actions. That wouldn't be fair. It was my fault. It was all my fault, Cabbie.

When I hit you, I wasn't hitting you. I'm sure it felt like I was hitting you—I remember you vomited, which means my fist must've plunged deep into your solar plexus, sending a signal to your stomach to evacuate, a fight response. You should be proud of that, Cabbie. You're a fighter, just like me. But know that in that moment I wasn't hitting you, I was hitting myself. I was hitting who I was, who I might be.

That night was my first back in the States after a third tour to Iraq. I was leaving the Marine Corps in a month. The people I'd known and loved, they were disappearing, some were leaving on other deployments, some were dying, Cabbie—have you known people who've died? You must have, everyone does—and there I was, helpless, waiting, no one back home to love me, to crawl in bed with at night. I'd ruined that, ruined everything. That's why I kept grabbing the dancers, Cabbie. I wasn't trying to be lewd or anything, I just wanted a connection. I just wanted someone to tell me I'd be all right. Maybe that's what I was trying to do with you, Cabbie.

When you showed up, Cabbie, I was crying and screaming at the bouncers who threw me out, and my brother had just punched my uncle in the face hard enough to buckle his knees and send him to the asphalt. Their relationship is only now starting to heal, this many years later. It was like a ripple in a pond, Cabbie, but instead of a pebble it was me and I soaked everyone in proximity, tore down my family like a tsunami.

I was out of my head, Cabbie. Can you imagine that? I think you can. You must go out of your head, too. Where are you from, Cabbie? You had an accent, but I don't remember it. A quick Internet search tells me there are a quite a few Somali cabdrivers in Southern California. Are you one of them? How strange that would be. It seems I can't go anywhere without running into someone whose country the Marine Corps hasn't fucked over. I think we would get along under different circumstances, Cabbie. I'm usually a generous tipper and a decent conversationalist. I'm a blue-collar kind of guy; I appreciate how hard you must work.

*Cabbie, I know I didn't want to pay, I know I didn't want to get
out of your taxi, I know I hit you unprovoked in the gut, and you
got stiffed on the bill, but for the first time since joining the Marines
I didn't laugh about it the next day. I knew that nothing would be
the same and I think I owe you something for that—not apologies,
but thanks. I think maybe I did all that not because I was drunk
and angry and looking for a fight but because I felt like you wanted
to get rid of me, too, Cabbie. I can't help wondering how things
could've been different. If you see this, write back and tell me which
knee my uncle kept moaning about and how my brother got me to
stop attacking you. Maybe we can get a coffee, or I can at least give
you the fifty dollars I owe.*

Leaving Our Mark

IN THE WEEKS BEFORE I end my active service, Chris is on restriction—like house arrest without the stylish ankle bracelet. Even though I've been mostly sober (not counting a cycle of steroids, one bottle of stateside Jameson sent while deployed, and the night of my homecoming) for the past six months and I know I shouldn't drink, we get wasted in our barracks room, and then later decide to celebrate my homecoming by attempting to burn down the thirty-feet-high diving platform just off Cristianitos Road.

In the driver's seat of my Jeep—now our getaway car—with the engine idling and the lights off, I'm waiting for Chris while he spills five gallons of gasoline over the water-bloated wood and molded Astroturf of the diving structure. I am starting to sober up and I think this is a bad idea. I think I'm going to fall right back into the same deep end I just pulled myself out of six months ago. I think about leaving—gunning the Jeep and driving back home to Indiana to forget the last four years have happened.

Futures roll out in front of me: I could be a teacher, a drunk, a coward, a lover, a student, a criminal, a husband, a child, a father. There are too many variables in the future. Too many unknowns. I panic.

I am putting the Jeep into drive when Chris comes running and hops the fence, seems to hurdle all eight feet of the fucker, and jumps in the passenger seat. I nail the gas and we fly into the darkness, into the coastal hills. Our laughs reek of beer and whiskey. We drive blacked out over rutted roads, up berms, through thickets of wild fennel giving off black licorice stink. A pale orange glow from the platform flicks in the rearview and I think we did it. We destroyed something—accomplished something we set out to do. We gave ourselves a mission and the mission is complete.

It is a perfect moment and I see one final future: The Jeep tips, bursts into flames, turns us to ashes along with the diving platform.

I want to die—not out of depression or because I feel horrible, but because I feel alive, and I think this is the only way I'll ever feel alive again. I think, Maybe I'll just angle up a hill and come down too steep, maybe I'll just take my hands off the wheel and everything will end and I won't have to worry about failing in the future.

We make it back to the room, have some beers, and fall asleep.

In the morning, during PT, I see the wood isn't even scorched.

Soapbox

Rifling through old gear and notes late one night when I can't sleep, I stumble across Past-me. He's mouthy and cock-struts into the room, fresh from basic training. I immediately hate him. I don't know why, but I know it's not his fault.

Past-me: Well first of all I want to say, thanks for your service—it's good to know we live.

Me: I'm not sure how I should respond to that.

Past-me: To "thank you"?

Me: Well if I say "you're welcome," it implies agreement and belief.

Past-me: Belief in what?

Me: Belief that we ever did something worth giving thanks for. And if I said thank you in response to your thanks it might indicate that I appreciate or even care that you want to thank me. That somehow I'm thankful you've taken the time out of your day to thank me for things you don't know anything about—yet. I mean, we could've murdered an entire Iraqi village or raped and pillaged, and here you are thanking me.

Past-me: But do we? Did we?

Me: Of course not. You don't know this yet, but most people you thank for their service joke about killing babies and fucking their mothers. They have wet dreams about pink mist, about shake 'n' bakes, about enfilade fire. They're chronic masturbators, philanderers, and alcoholics. They wish for five hundred-pounders to drop on mosques just so the call to prayer will stop, they take bumps of coke before they get behind the gun, and smoke weed in the corners of FOBs to even out. They shoot dogs out of boredom.

Past-me: I mean war is hell, right? But we probably did some pretty cool shit. Firefights, rescue missions—you don't think we should be thanked for that? For our service to the country? Hey, how many medals do we have?

Me: None of that happens. You'll feel so ashamed that none of it happens that you'll lie and say we did do that stuff. You'll lie for a long time, and you'll lie so much that you'll start to believe the lies.

Past-me: Sounds hard to live with.

Me: It keeps me up nights. I don't sleep well.

Past-me: We have posttraumatic stress, or whatever? Nightmares?

Me: Everyone has PTSD, and if I have nightmares now they're guilt-based.

Past-me: Jesus Christ, you sound like a real civvy-boy pussy piece of shit. If we weren't in any kind of firefight and you never killed anyone, what kind of nightmares do you have?

Me: For a long time after the first deployment I had a dream where I was court-martialed for not doing my job as a rear Humvee passenger and not grabbing a gunner's legs to keep him in the truck when we got hit by a culvert bomb—you're going to get hit by a culvert bomb, by the way—I was supposed to grab his legs and pull him down.

Past-me: Well from what it sounds like maybe we deserve a nightmare or two.

Me: Wait until you start having the recurring dream where you're being torn apart by decaying dogs.

Past-me: You really fucked us over, huh? So much for being a hero.

Me: What's your definition of hero?

Past-me: Someone who acts selflessly in the face of adversity. Not someone who shoots dogs and compulsively masturbates.

Me: Would you say that someone who gets a leg blown off in war is a hero?

Past-me: Sure.

Me: What if the day before he got his leg blown off he pissed on the corpse of someone he killed?

Past-me: Well . . .

Me: So you use the word hero just like you thank people for their service.

Past–me: Well it's better than the way vets got treated when they got back from Vietnam.

Me: Enforcing the idea that every service member is a hero is dangerous. You're going to meet some tough Marines who did some real heroic shit, but I don't know if that makes them heroes. I don't know if anyone can ever really be a hero. I worry about long-term implications of calling everyone who serves in the military a hero.

Past–me: Oh my God. Is this really what I turn into? "I'm worried about long-term implications"? You're fucking whiny. Jesus.

Me: Are you done?

Past–me: Fine. Fuck. I'll bite, what kind of long-term implications?

Me: Like creating a generation of veterans who believe everything they did was good and that they really were defending the people of the United States and not oil interests. It feels like we're creating an army of fanatics.

Past–me: You don't believe America was at risk after September 11?

Me: I think we were able to combat that with increased airport security.

Past–me: But we had to get even.

Me: Beyond the fact that bin Laden wasn't in Iraq, I don't think we needed to go to war. Those countries simply didn't have the infrastructure to merit such a large-scale multiyear occupation.

Past-me: I live in the past—I'm eighteen. I just want to screw girls, get paid, and kill like I've been trained. You're saying 9/11 wasn't that big a deal? How did we get so brainwashed? Is that the kind of liberal commie pinko bullshit we learn in college?

Me: What the fuck? No. Also, you came home from school that day in September and complained there was nothing on television but the news. You told your—our—mom you didn't care when she called you crying her eyes out. Don't forget that.

Past-me: . . .

Me: Listen. Christ. I'm sorry, all right? It's not all bad.

Past-me: Yeah? How so?

Me: You're going to start to figure it out—your life. Our life. After some time as a horrible, thoughtless person, you'll start to be better. You'll appreciate hard work and loyalty and love. You'll quit smoking. You'll slow down. You'll think about the consequences of your actions. You'll question the motivations of others. After witnessing so much inequality and violence and pain you'll become more empathetic. You'll come out the other side of all this scuffed and jaded and angry, but you'll go to college and learn to use that anger. You'll learn to transform it into thought, into words. You'll start running to mitigate your trauma. You'll adopt a dog. You'll get married. You'll go to graduate school. You'll help people understand war. You'll help people.

Past-me: I guess that sounds okay. But I still don't get why you couldn't just say thank you.

A Real Boy

IF THERE'S ANYTHING I'VE LEARNED, it's to keep my hair long. It's the differentiating factor between the gung ho brainwashed eighteen-year-old I was when I joined and the civilian I desperately want to be. The high and tight is what people notice first, the thing that doesn't mesh with certain types of clothing (mainly anything not a uniform). People peg me immediately. They look at me and think, Jarhead. So I keep it long. I get a fingernail fade—if I'd enlisted two years later the style would be in vogue, the 1920s Dust Bowl cut. I don't shave on the weekends; two-day stubble does wonders. No one gives me a second look by Sunday evening. A friend's girlfriend says, I didn't think you were a Marine. I smile with pride.

Sometimes I find myself giving up and drinking at jarhead bars outside of base. I go with my platoon mates. I go and talk about fucking and fighting and shooting and drinking. Hard talk. I drink and drink until it feels like I'm downing in the booze. Until it feels like my liver is pickled and I spew my guts into a urinal because I can't find the toilet in the bathroom.

Then the bouncer tries to throw me out but one of my mates blindsides the man in the jaw and the bar is a wild rumpus with Benny Hill music blaring from the juke. There's screaming and yelling and punching and kicking and I see the bouncer who tried to haul me out lying on the floor, groaning, trying to get back on his feet until another of my mates runs over and field goals the man in the ribs, and I hear bones crack. My buddy's still kicking, slam dancing into the guy's gut and I watch until someone else broadsides him, and then they're tussling on the ground and I look around and there's an abandoned beer and my mouth is desert dry and tastes like vomit and so I drink it, and then I'm wandering around drinking abandoned beers until there are sirens in the distance.

It's a long walk to base and the lot of us are laughing and trying to show knotty faces to one another in the dark. There's a pool inside the gate, another half mile down the road, all lit bright blue with undulating shadows in the complete seaside desert darkness, just for us.

I'm naked, climbing a wooden ladder to the top of the thirty-feet-high platform used to simulate water entry from helicopters, which I tried to burn down a few weeks ago. The platform is covered in moldy stamped-down Astroturf that squeaks and slides under the balls of my feet. The others are in the water below, bobbing, floating on their backs, yelling at me through the dark.

They drunkenly sing running cadence, voices echoing off the wet concrete surrounding the pool. Through the rungs of the platform their faces blur into my drill instructor, into Sergeants Johnson and Carmichael and Mars, into Hashim Ibrahim Awad and Cheeks and Fisher and Lawrence, into faceless bar girls and my fiancée, into my family. When I reach the top of the platform and look down into the pool, the faces yell up at me. Jump, they say.

From the summit I can see the sixty miles to San Diego International Airport, where my plane is just landing on the tarmac four years ago. I can see my own past-face in the porthole—unlined, pale, nervous. I want to reach out for that face, grab it, and tell it . . . what? Nothing, I decide. I want to tell it nothing. Maybe I want to see the innocence destroyed because my own has been broken or maybe I realize that there's no point. I can talk at the face—at all the faces—tell them horror stories, make the boredom and jackassery a reality, show them loss and suicidal sadness, but it won't matter, just as it never has.

I leap into the dark, eyes shut, wind whirring over tiny hairs on my body. I fall for what seems like forever. Just when I think I sense water rushing toward me and hear the voices of my buddies growing louder I keep falling.

So I will time to speed up; pray yell beg threaten bargain. But time chooses when it will and won't move. I know that from minutes that felt like hours on the quarterdeck in basic training and from the hours that felt like days on sunbaked roofs or slogging through shit fields and rolling down pock-marked roads at two miles per hour and from the days that turned into years that ended up feeling like decades, and now I'm some decrepit ancient thing falling and falling, expecting a bottom, hoping that maybe it won't be a hard landing and I'll walk away intact, wet feet padding the asphalt, teeth chattering against the cool coastal night.

Even after I hit the water and the chlorine burns my eyes, thins my hair, dries my skin to ash, I'm still falling. In that moment I don't know there's not a bottom. I think that I've landed, but I'm not on solid ground. Years from now when I've been out and I'm married and I'm in grad school and I'm trying to forget those times I chugged whiskey and fought and was shot at and exploded and lived in a hole and hated life and hated everyone and hated myself and shot mongrel dogs and screwed anything that moved and smoked two packs a day and hazed new joins and ran until I threw up because I was still drunk from the night before and made my family cry I'll realize that I'll never be a civilian—that I'm still tumbling and twisting through the air waiting to land.

End of Active Service
Health Assessment

COMPARED PRIOR TO YOUR ENLISTMENT how would you rate your health in general now?

- o Outstanding
- o Wonderful
- o Terrific
- o Super
- o Excellent
- o First-rate
- o Very good
- o Good
- o Somewhat good
- o Better than OK
- o OK

- Decent
- Fine
- Satisfactory
- Reasonable
- Adequate
- Suitable
- Fair
- Less than fair, but not bad
- Not too bad. I can't complain, I guess.

Acknowledgments

I OWE A DEBT OF gratitude to the following people, without whom this book would not exist:

The magazine editors who gave some of these pieces early, wonderful homes.

The fantastic creative writing and English faculty at Oregon State University—Marjorie Sandor, Keith Scribner, Susan Jackson Rodgers, and Neil Davison—who brought me back to humanity through writing and literature.

The faculty in the graduate creative writing program at Miami University—Margaret Luongo, for your friendship and guidance; Eric Goodman, for not bullshitting a bullshitter; Jody Bates, for fostering in me a love for speculative fiction, which inspired many nonfiction tales in this book; Brian Roley, for helping me fully understand what I was trying to do. To my graduate cohort for your thoughtful, kind, and astute readings of my work. Without you these would still be bar stories.

To Stefanie Dunning, for her course on trauma. It provided clarity, purpose, and depth.

The folks at Words After War—Brandon Willitts, Matt Gallagher, and John Sheehy—for accepting me to the summer writing intensive at Marlboro College. It kept me writing when I thought I was done. To the vets and civilians I met there—especially Francisco Martinezcuello, Tricia Theis, and Matthew Robinson—for your honesty, counsel, humor, and motivation on early-morning runs.

Josh Friedman, Tim Weiner, and the entire advisory board at the Carey Institute for Global Good's Logan Nonfiction Fellowship for taking a chance on a creative nonfiction writer, for a beautiful space in which to finish my book, and for asking me hard questions over bourbon and not accepting easy answers. To my cohort there as well—especially Susannah Breslin, Justin Cohen, and Camas Davis—for your readership, guidance, encouragement, and willingness to perform an inebriated Marine Corps Daily Seven routine.

The lovely people at Artist Trust in Seattle, for believing in my work enough to deem it deserving of a Grant for Artist Projects that kept me and mine in the black.

Bill Clegg at the Clegg Agency, for reading what I wrote and thinking it needed a bigger life, and for introducing me to Chris.

My agent, Chris Clemans (Holy shit. Is this real life? Yes. Because of you.), for being a thoughtful and encouraging reader, a competent (and gentle) editor, and a patient human being and friend.

Anton Mueller, my editor at Bloomsbury, for getting it, for your light hand, and for telling me I wasn't finished.

My 3/5 brothers—especially John Ta, Adam Flynn, and Charlie Beaston—for the honor and privilege to serve alongside you. Get some.

My family, for your love, patience, help, loaner cars, places to crash, and not laughing at me when I told you I wanted to be a writer.

My wife, for coming with me on this weird trip, for helping me tell these stories, and for knowing and loving every version of me.

A Note on the Author

Matt Young holds an MA in Creative Writing from
Miami University and is the recipient of fellowships with
Words After War and the Carey Institute for Global Good.
His work can be found in *Tin House, Word Riot,*
the *Rumpus,* and elsewhere. He is a combat veteran
and lives in Olympia, Washington, where
he teaches composition.